THE TECHNIQUES OF

PAINTING

THE TECHNIQUES OF

PAINTING

DORI WATSON

GALAHAD BOOKS · NEW YORK CITY

To

CHARLES

il tempo passa

and prayerfully always will

with joy and affection

Also by Dori Watson (with Phil Brodatz):
The Human Form in Action and Repose (Reinhold, 1966)
The Elements of Landscape (Reinhold, 1968)

Library of Congress Catalog Card Number: 73-90505
ISBN 0-88365-123-8
Designed by Myron S. Hall III
Line drawings by the author
Printed in the United States of America
This edition published by arrangement with Van
Nostrand Reinhold Company

I would like to express my gratitude to the many people who have helped in one way or another, to make this book possible. My first and greatest debt is to Professor Mary Holmes. Surely I would have been less deeply involved in art — and surely this book would not have been written — had I not had the great privilege of studying under so inspired a teacher. Among my colleagues I want especially to thank Sterling McIlhany for sharing his thoughts on art in delightful conversation over the years — a dialogue that enriches and clarifies writing in a way that cannot be measured. I am also particularly in debt to Stan and Pat Fillmore, dear friends who offered support as well as professional help throughout. Others, too, have been helpful and, although they are too numerous to name, they know who they are and that they have my heartfelt thanks.

The task of gathering the picture material was made lighter by the kind cooperation of a host of people, and for each photograph I would like to express my thanks. I am particularly grateful to Simone Gossner; Jane Nitterauer of the Albright-Knox Gallery; Janet Snow of the Art Reference Bureau; Bess Barzansky; Loyce Porter of the Museum of Fine Arts of Boston; Dr. Sherman Lee, Director of The Cleveland Museum of Art; Professoressa Evelina Borea, Director, Gabinetto Fotografico, Soprintendenza alle Gallerie di Firenze; René Faille of Giraudon; Mrs. Gylbert Adams of the Solomon R. Guggenheim Museum; Antoinette Kraushaar of the Kraushaar Galleries; Mariol Gallichio of the Marlborough-Gerson Gallery; Molly Schirm of the Midtown Galleries; Nada Saporiti of The Metropolitan Museum of Art; Richard L. Tooke of The Museum of Modern Art, New York; William W. Morrison of the National Gallery of Art, Washington, D.C.; Mary Ratcliffe of the Lee Nordness Galleries; Anna Horan of the Philadelphia Museum of Art; Eleanore Saidenberg of the Saidenberg Gallery; Maxine Novek of the Allan Stone Galleries; and to Mrs. Denny Judson of the Whitney Museum of American Art. I am grateful, also to three artists, Karl Zerbe, Russell Woody, and Frank Cicero, who lent special assistance in providing illustrations of their work.

Crown Publishers kindly allowed the use of the quotations by Orozco and Siqueiros from *The Mexican Muralists* by Alma Reed.

The business of producing a book involves a great many persons who go to work after the author has finished and settled back to relax. As a two-fingered typist who regards the typewriter as a natural foe, my gratitude to Robert Johnson is boundless. He undertook the tremendous job of typing the manuscript and the correspondence, cheerfully unravelling my scrawls. I am grateful to Nancy C. Newman for her editorial work, and to designer Myron S. Hall III, who did so very much to create a book of great visual appeal.

Acknowledgments

Contents

In *The Artist and His Studio* Rembrandt van Ryn (1609-1669) gives us a glimpse of himself as a young man at work, holding brushes, palette, and mahlstick (a stick used as a hand rest).

In a painting, the artist translates thoughts and emotions into visual form. His craftsmanship is handmaiden to his efforts, serving well if with it he handles skillfully the materials that are best suited to expressing what he has to say.

This book is about painting media and techniques. By media, we mean the *substances* — the paint, wax, or other vehicle of color — used by the artist to achieve his effects; by techniques, we mean the *ways* in which he manipulates the media to achieve these effects. Before taking up the specific media, however, we should assess the importance of technique in the broad sense of the word. Technique *is* important — so much so that it is easy to ascribe too much significance to it. But it is never technique that determines the greatness of a work of art, even though it is the vehicle of artistic expression and to a great extent determines the "look" of the artist's work.

Beyond the technique used, whatever it may be, lies the idea, the inspiration, the human statement to be made — the reason for the painting. No amount of facility with any technique — or all of them — can supplant this; in painting, as in any other art, superb technique can never take the place of having something to say. Lack of technique will never seriously thwart expression (though it may slow it up a bit); having something to say, the artist will either find or invent a way of saying it.

The fact that the artist has something to say should be touched upon briefly, because it relates to the raison d'être of art and the nature of creativity. Not to mention it would be like putting a bit of sawdust under a microscope in order to better understand a tree before ever having seen one.

Artists have had something to say and found means of expressing it from the dawn of humanity. Art began when man first sought to bring some sort of order into the world about him (actually, it marked the beginning of humanity). This meant an application of intelligence to the disorder of experience to make it manageable and coherent. Whenever man has achieved order and form

Introduction: Art and Technique

In its art a culture expresses its spirit and values. The bas-reliefs of the Assyrians, who were called the "scourge of the ancient world," depicted their exploits in war and peace. All, like this scene of men setting out to hunt with nets and dogs, convey a sense of brute strength and ferocity.

in his surroundings, his life, his thoughts and beliefs, he has been creative. Where this order and form are apparent, it is art, whether it is a plowed field, a poem, a religion, or a law.

Seeing art in the context of its real function and value rather than as some peripheral, impractical indulgence separate from the serious business of living is basic to an understanding of the nature of art — and life. It begins to explain why art is, and always has been, a central and integral part of the human experience. If we regard works of art as an extension and expression of the urge toward order, control, and understanding, it is easier to see why they have, in various circumstances, been worshiped, deliberately destroyed, or avidly collected. It is easier to see, too, why whole societies and civilizations are sometimes understood and frequently judged on the basis of the works of art they created. In their art is the crystallization of all that they worshiped, feared, or strived for.

Taking his cue from the forms of life and thought around him, the artist sums up for all to see just how his time interprets reality. To put it another way, art is the reality of an age isolated and given clear and succinct expression. In art, intangible values are given tangible form. For example, a glance at what the artists of ancient Assyria rendered over and over again reveals an almost overwhelming delight in brute strength, cruelty, bloodshed, and the destruction of the weak by which their nation survived (and gained the reputation "scourge of the ancient world"). Bulging, hard muscularity, cruel leers, and impaled victims are not only depicted in the bas-reliefs of warring exploits. In times of peace, the Assyrian view of the world was not much different. Works of art show the princely pursuit of pleasure — the lion hunt, mainly. Variations include horses clawed and hamstrung, and lions speared and dragging their entrails; all reflect the same violent, brutal, material values. Assyrian artists produced, with singular steadfastness, meticulous and masterly interpretations of what their society demanded and delighted in. They didn't render subjects such as the life-after-death, making love, or baking bread. This is not because such things didn't exist; they were simply irrelevant.

Through most of the history of art, artists have func-

tioned within particular traditions. The Assyrians' work resembled that of their fellow artists, and, because it clearly reflected universally accepted values and beliefs, their work was understood as readily as their own spoken language. When there is only one tradition, there is no problem of understanding.

Unlike the Assyrian artists — or any artists of the past — we live at a time in which barriers between peoples and traditions are being deliberately torn down in the interest of common understanding and survival. The full study of man has embraced and made familiar virtually every culture of the past and every extant artistic expression. For the first time, the artist, whose concern is (as it has always been) the interpretation of reality, has an overwhelming number of possibilities to choose from. Now he must decide what is *most* real and how it may best be expressed in his art. Is reality the surface appearance of things? Personality? Suffering? Mechanization and dehumanization? God? The "death of God"? Atomic structure? Hot dogs and Coca-Cola? Simply the act of painting?

Despite this range of choices, art that is based on "realism" as defined during the sixteenth century is the art that is best understood and popularly accepted today. Yet many artists have long since reshaped or departed from this "realism" in search of a way to express the realities that sustain — or threaten — life now. Thus, we are confronted by a bewildering array of modern and traditional styles — a situation that leaves many of us gasping, faintly angered, and thoroughly convinced that the artist has no notion what he is doing.

The artist *does* know what he is doing. However, the present situation places him in the rather uncomfortable seat of Damocles. His royal banquet — his personal freedom of expression — is spread before him, but the sword hangs above him. His works are no longer always understood; he shoulders the burden of discerning reality for himself, and, perhaps most galling of all, he notices that the door opened to personal expression and understanding may admit an army of pretenders not particularly concerned with the integrity and human significance of art, who blithely substitute tricks for truth, fads for the search for reality.

Nevertheless, there has never been so much room for

Every art medium has its own inherent qualities as well as a wide expressive range, as is illustrated by these two crayon drawings, *Old Man with Bowed Head* (above) by Vincent van Gogh (1853-1890) and *Reclining Nude* (opposite) by Aristide Maillol (1861-1944). In both studies the medium is used with utmost integrity — the crayon remains crayon; it is not disguised to resemble something else — yet in expression the two drawings are entirely different. In van Gogh's hand the crayon conveys the shadowed depths of human despair; Maillol produced a lovely study of depersonalized, ideal form.

experimentation, such latitude for expression, as for the serious artist today. He may do whatever he wants to do. There is no subject matter he may not use — a rose, a gouty toe, or nothing at all beyond his own dialogue with his materials. He may make a sublime statement or toy with sheer pornography. He is not constrained by requirements of content or meaning other than those he establishes for himself, because there is no single set of values. He can choose from all the media that have ever been used; he can employ any traditional technique or paint on a curtain with shoe polish if he wishes.

Presuming there is serious purpose, the contemporary artist can produce significant works of art. But since so much of what he does is a matter of choice, he should be equipped to make the most sensitive, informed choice possible. The only alternative is to be a true primitive who through an honest lack of awareness sees no choice at all.

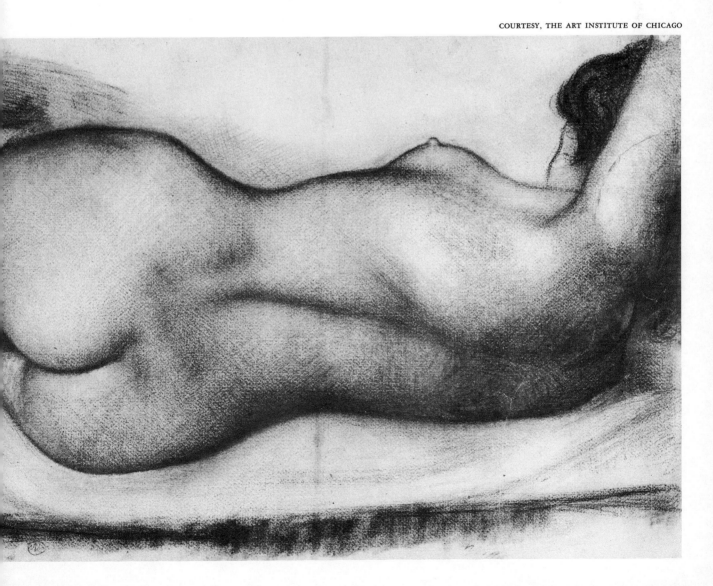

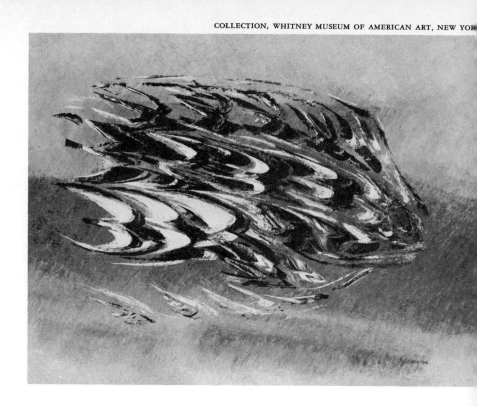

These four works of similar subjects by the same artist, Morris Graves, demonstrate how the medium contributes to the effects of a work. On the left, *Shore Birds*, a sketch done in *sumi* ink; above, *Flight of Plovers*, an oil painting.

The choices made by the artist revolve around what he says and how he says it. One part of "how he says it" is the medium he selects, and that is the province of this book. It involves more than recipes and step-by-step instructions. To choose the most appropriate medium for the intended expression, and to use it most effectively, depends upon familiarity with media and techniques per se. It includes an awareness of the origins of media and the uses to which they have been put. Thus, a discussion of technique moves into seemingly tangential areas. It may include a generous portion of art history, since what artists have said and done from time to time has both determined and been determined by the technique involved. It may even bring into the account such factors as geography and climate, where these have determined the materials available and the methods used.

14

Above, *Spirit Bird*, tempera on a gold ground;
right, *Blind Bird*, a gouache painting.

Painting is not a simple matter of knowing the specific formula of a given medium. It may be to know and embrace a technique perfectly, or it may mean to depart from it into seemingly devious paths. Either extreme is possible, as well as any number of variations between. The gravest responsibility of the artist is to know what he is doing — and why. If he chooses encaustic or fresco, he must know why he is doing so. And if he puts aside all of the time-sanctioned media, he should do so knowing their potentials and limitations. This requires familiarity not only with specific recipes but also with the forms and functions for which they were evolved and to which they were subsequently applied. Such an acquaintance with the arsenal of his art will give the painter some notion of where to begin to say what he wants to say.

15

Realism infused with serenity and order characterize the paintings of Johannes Vermeer (1632-1675).
Illustrated is his *Young Woman with a Water Jug*, an oil painting.

1.

The Art of Painting

Many of us cherish a number of ideas about what painting is. A painting is something produced by an artist, and it is meant to be framed, hung on a wall, and admired. Within its borders we expect the artist to depict recognizable objects — things that clearly refer to counterparts in the real world. And we expect him to do so in such a way that the picture is pleasing to look at. There is nothing whatsoever wrong with these ideas when they are applied to some paintings, for many were created with these very ideas in mind. Moreover, these ideas have been eloquently expressed by a variety of authorities:

"To paint is to be able to portray upon a flat surface any visible thing whatsoever that may be chosen," Albrecht Dürer said. And in a letter to a patron, to whom Dürer hoped to sell a painting, the artist wrote, "If a proper frame were put on it, it would be a beautiful painting. . . ."

In the words of another Renaissance artist, Leon Battista Alberti, "the grace and beauty of things is much to be sought after. To ensure this, I think there is no more appropriate and sure way than to follow nature, recalling in what way nature, the marvellous maker of things, has composed the surfaces well in beautiful bodies."

Speaking of Tintoretto's art, the seventeenth-century Italian essayist Carlo Ridolfi wrote, "One of Tintoretto's attributes, praised by many an artist, was his ability to imagine the effect that a painting would make when hung in a particular place."

These statements hint at and apply to a definition of painting in the Renaissance tradition (and hence relate to much of the painting done from the fifteenth through the nineteenth centuries). It became *the* definition of painting because during the Renaissance artists for the first time started probing their art with words and recording their aims and intentions. This twofold process ultimately produced a self-conscious aim, on the part of artists, to create Art, and, on the part of everyone else, a reliance on explanations and definitions of what Art is — and what is Good Art. In popular thought, painting thus came to mean the "fine art" of making pictures that are realistic and pleasing to look at — a definition well exemplified by such a work as *Young Woman With a Water Jug* by Vermeer.

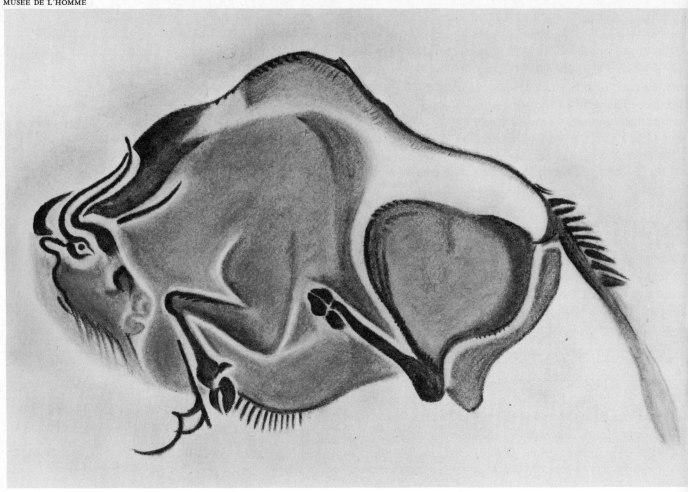

Images such as this bison from the caves of Altamira, in Spain, were an integral part of Cro-Magnon man's pre-hunt ritual. It was the artist's task to create a likeness that captured the essence of the quarry.

Yet what has such a definition to do with the painting of other times, other places? What, for example, has it to do with the statement, "Painting is voyaging into the night, one knows not where . . . ," made by Robert Motherwell, one of the foremost painters of our own time? Not, in fact, very much. To hope to grasp all of painting in terms of that one familiar notion is like trying to catch a tiger in a mousetrap. So, painting as art must be more than we thought it was, and our ideas about art, consequently, must be expanded considerably. Happily enough the process is additive rather than subtractive. That which is familiar and therefore dear is not threatened. One's own beloved neighborhood is no less appealing after travels abroad. Paradoxically, its own peculiar characteristics may be savored and more keenly appreciated when other neighborhoods in distant places have also, even briefly, become "home." Of course, it occasionally happens that the familiar, beloved neighborhood does not look quite so good after we have encountered other possibilities, and so we may move to some new place, which may prove even more dear. Either way, the definition of "home" has become larger, not smaller.

Sixteen thousand years lie between the Cro-Magnon hunter-artists who created pictures of beasts of prey deep in the caves of Altamira, Lascaux, and Font-de-Gaume and the medieval monk-artists who illuminated manuscripts in the scriptoria of monasteries all across Europe. During that long time man moved a great distance, through ten millennia of shadowy prehistory and six millennia of complex cultural development.

Whatever may separate them — and certainly much

A tenth-century artist decorated a manuscript with this miniature showing St. Luke the Evangelist at work on his gospel. The task of copying and illuminating religious texts was an expression of devotion and an avenue of Christian service for medieval monks.

19

does — Cro-Magnon man and the medieval monk possessed in common their attitude toward their painting. They did not consider it art. Painting was but one of the many tasks required by the business of living in their respective times. For the one it was a necessary prelude to a successful hunt, since he considered the image of the prey powerful magic; to stalk and kill the effigy ritually gave the hunter control over the animal even before he encountered it. For the other it was an expression of faith that all of life, here and hereafter, was subject to the Word of God, in which lay man's only hope and salvation. Each, in different fashion, was creating out of necessity; neither was intentionally producing works of art.

The works that fill museums all over the world have been removed from their original contexts, gathered together, and framed or put on pedestals, and by the process have clearly become "art" — or, more precisely, "fine art." Certainly we are fortunate that these works which are so precious a part of our human heritage have been thus preserved and cared for and, what is more, that they are displayed to public view. Yet when we see them in a museum, we must remember that "fine art" is quite a modern notion; in earlier times the production of art was simply a necessary vocation. Until

the fifteenth century, painters did not paint paintings — they painted walls, altarpieces, pots, book illuminations, cupboards. They never created their works apart from a specific commission or use. There was no such thing as "art for art's sake." To illustrate this: the Greeks of fifth-century Athens, who created such masterpieces as the pediment sculpture of the Parthenon, had no word for "art" in their language. (The word that came closest was *techne*, or "craftsmanship," which referred to the skill of making anything — from a pot to a poem.)

The cave painter, the Greek sculptor, and the medieval monk would be astonished and mystified to see their work as we see it now. For our own part, if we could, for a brief moment, divest the works of their gilt frames and imposing pedestals and see them in use as they were meant to be seen, we would learn a great deal. We would understand that beyond being something more or less aesthetically pleasing to us, each work is the product of a human hand and mind, created to serve a human need. As such it reflects a particular set of human values and constitutes a statement about life and reality. Let us mentally take these works from their frames and pedestals and explore a few of the myriad functions they were created to serve, for these determined what the artist did — and how he did it.

As painting and sculpture were elevated to the status of "fine art" — a concept evolved during the Renaissance — the works of major artists were avidly sought by royal patrons and wealthy commoners. The treasures they accumulated formed the basis for most of the great national galleries and public museums. For Americans unable to visit Paris (and also to help finance his telegraph), Samuel F.B. Morse (1791-1872) did this vast oil painting entitled *The Exhibition Gallery of The Louvre*. It shows the Salon Carée as it looked in 1829, with a display of nearly forty masterpieces (among them Leonardo's *Mona Lisa*, Raphael's *La Belle Jardiniere*, Titian's *Entombment*, and Poussin's *Diogenes*.

20

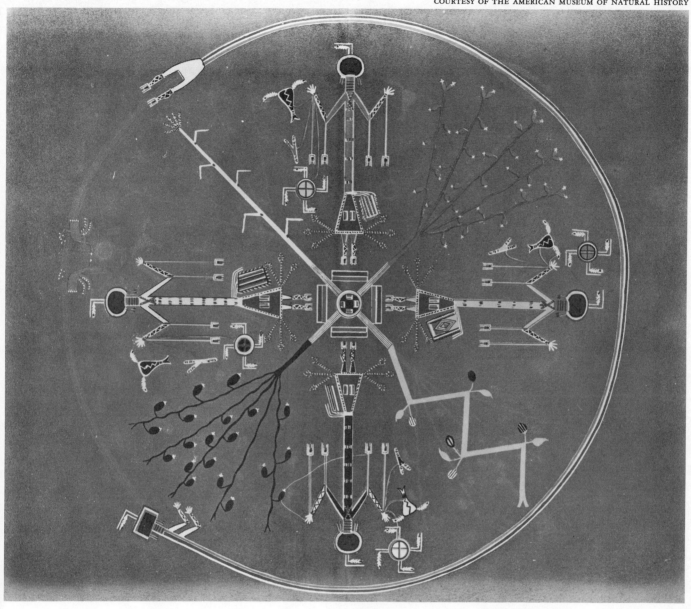

The Mountain Chant, a Navajo sand-painting design. This art form was inseparably bound to ritual.

MAGIC AND RITUAL

Painting done for magic or ritual purposes is not confined to the Old Stone Age cave art; it can be found in many other primitive cultures. An example of ritual art practiced into the twentieth century is Navajo sand painting. To the accompaniment of incantations, intricate signs and symbols were outlined in colored sand on the ground, where they remained throughout the day while ceremonial chants and dances were offered. To be effective, the ritual had to be finished and the sand painting scattered to the winds before sunset. The painting was not only a focus for the ritual but an embodiment of the prayers which, to reach the spirits, had to be literally scattered forth. Such art has been called "mystic," for it derives from a view of the world in which the seen and the unseen are equally real and inseparable.

INSTRUCTION TOWARD MORALITY

If a painting is worth a thousand words, as has been said, then one might expect to find all manner of instruction and information communicated graphically. And indeed, human behavior and conduct have been a fruitful motivation for art. Sometimes human morality and perfectibility have actually constituted the core of religion, as was the case in ancient Greece. Religion was centered upon human life. To this end, a great many of the myths graphically described man's capacity for good and evil and drew exceedingly vivid morals, especially on the latter. For his disobedience and ambition, Icarus plunged to his death. Midas, for his greed, was granted the "golden touch" that transformed even his food into lumps of metal, and for his stupidity, his ears were transformed into those of an ass. Narcissus perished from self-love, unable to tear himself away from the pool where he languished over his own reflection. Actaeon was turned into a stag by Artemis and devoured by his hunting hounds because he accidentally came upon the goddess bathing in a spring — such was the

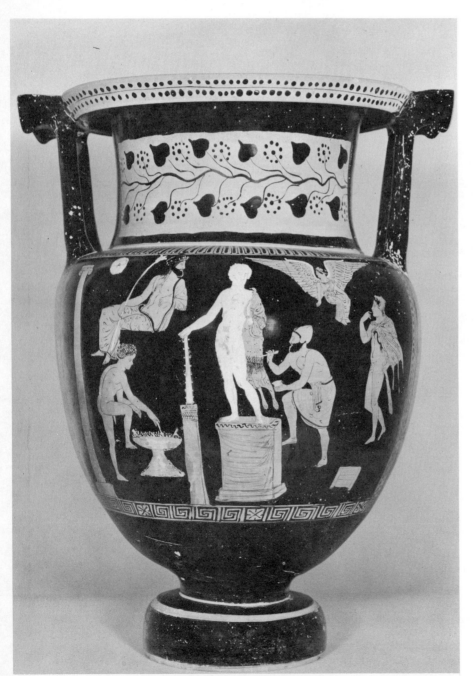

The scene on this terracotta Apulian vase of the fourth century B.C. shows an artist painting a statue of Herakles. In classical Greece, art was considered to be one embodiment of the ideals and excellence to be striven for in human life.

dire punishment for a mortal who dared confront a god unbidden.

The noble virtues, too, were clearly told and frequently personified in the figures of gods and heroes. Beauty, strength, wisdom, truth, courage, fidelity, and honor were extolled, and man's duty was to cultivate them. Of the paintings, only those done on pottery have survived. Utensils of remarkable beauty, they carried graphic reminders of the excellence to be striven for by man.

Art has long been a vehicle for moral instruction, graphically presenting not only the noble virtues but also the high cost of wrongdoing or dishonor. Below, the *Death of Actaeon*, on a Greek vase (detail).

RELIGIOUS IMAGES

With the conscious separation of the seen and the unseen came organized religions and a new role for art. The natural and the spiritual worlds were perceived as distinct phenomena, and the spiritual sphere was developed, among other things, as an explanation of life and the natural world. Art then served and expressed religious beliefs in a variety of ways.

The ancient Egyptians were preoccupied with extending earthly life beyond the grave, and a complex system of rituals, as well as a style of architecture, painting, and sculpture, were evolved to this end. Of greatest importance was ensuring that the "ka" — each person's life force, or a sort of spiritual twin — forever have a place to reside. The first dwelling place was the actual body of the deceased, which was mummified to preserve it from the destructive forces of time. Should the mummy inadvertently be destroyed, an accompanying statue of the deceased served for the ka. In the tomb-chapels, paintings or painted bas-reliefs depicted, among other things, food offerings, so that the deceased would have sustenance in the next world.

These paintings were not meant to be viewed, but rather actually to *be* what they represented, and this purpose established the conventions that were assiduously followed by Egyptian artists for three thousand years. The conventions may seem awkward to us at first, particularly if we assume the Egyptian artists were aiming at "realism." But the Egyptian artist was not remotely concerned with rendering things as they appear. He was concerned with their identity, so he showed their clearest characteristics. This sometimes meant selecting and combining different viewing angles: for example, among the offerings in the painting from Nakht's tomb, shown below, the large, circular loaves of bread and the isosceles-triangle-shaped shat-cakes are depicted as if seen from above; the baskets of figs, the bunches of grapes and onions, and the calf's head and shank are shown in profile. Similarly, in dealing with the human figure, the artist took each part separately. The head, legs, and feet are most distinctive in profile view, but the eyes, shoulders, and torso are most completely defined when seen "head on."

Since the Egyptian artistic conventions were evolved to convey identity rather than impressions, the rendering of space or perspective and the ephemeral effects of light and shadow was irrelevant. The offerings, laid out on a flat surface, are shown in the painting as in an upright ground plan, with nearby objects at the bottom and those farther away at the top. Scale is used to convey relative importance (rather than distance, as in "realistic" paintings). Importance is a conceptual matter, not a visual one — the nobleman in the painting from Luxor dwarfs his wife not because he actually was so much larger than she but because he was of far greater consequence.

Centuries after the eclipse of ancient Egypt, the pur-

PHOTOGRAPH BY EGYPTIAN EXPEDITION, THE METROPOLITAN MUSEUM OF ART

Egyptian painting served a religious function, perpetuating earthly realities into eternity. Every Egyptian looked forward to the moment when he would stand before the gods, see his heart weighed, and hear Thoth declare, "No evil has been found in him . . .," to which the gods would answer, "Grant that he be given the bread in the presence of Osiris, and a field in the Field of Peace like the followers of Horus." To this end artistic conventions were developed that translated the fleeting experiences of life into timeless forms. It was an art never to be viewed once the tomb was sealed. Opposite, a table of offerings, detail of wall painting from the tomb of Nakht. Above, a nobleman and his wife from a tomb at Luxor.

25

poses of art in another religion, Christianity, were enumerated by the Council of Nicaea in 787 A.D. It was said that the images of Christ, the Virgin, the angels, and the saints should be displayed in churches and elsewhere: "For by so much more frequently as they are seen in artistic representation, by so much more readily are men lifted up to the memory of their prototypes and to a longing after them: and to these be given due salvation and honorable reverence, not indeed the true worship of faith which pertains only to the divine nature, but to these as to the figure of the precious and life-giving Cross and to the book of the Gospels, and to the other holy objects incense and lights may be offered according to ancient pious custom. For the honor which is paid to the image passes to that which the image represents, and he who reveres the image reveres in it the subject represented."

Actually, this doctrine reflects only one side of a bitter controversy that raged over the use of images in worship. The aversion for religious images, inherited from Judaism by Christianity and shared by other religions, was based on the recognition that images have a potency or magic all their own, and may usurp the wor-

shiper's reverence, thus turning him toward idolatry. Buddhism forbade representations of Buddha and the Buddhist saints — a ban that was respected for five hundred years. Both Judaism and Mohammedanism have held steadfastly firm against sacred images; Buddhism and Christianity have not.

In the service of Christianity, painting found many uses. Artists were called upon to decorate church walls, altarpieces, and small panels that in early Christian and Byzantine churches were hung on the screen dividing the sanctuary from the nave of the church. Painters illuminated manuscripts and produced designs for enamelwork, textiles, and banners to be carried in religious processions. The paintings served, as they still do, as a means of instruction and a focus for devotion.

Reproduced here are two interpretations of an event from the life of St. Francis, one painted around 1235, the other a century later. Although both depict the same event in the saint's life and serve the same religious functions of edification and inspiration, they are utterly different. In three thousand years, the Egyptians did not alter their painting conventions so drastically as the conventions behind these two Christian paintings changed in less than one century. Why should this be so?

The reason is that every work of art is created within an entire context of human understanding and experience. When a society remains relatively unchanged, the art that expresses its views and values does not change. Broadly speaking, this was the case over an astonishing long period in ancient Egypt. But such has not often been the case, and it certainly has not been so in modern European history. Between the twelfth and fifteenth centuries occurred the transition from the Middle Ages to the Renaissance, and with it the beginning of the modern age. Egon Friedell, in his remarkable *Cultural History of the Modern Age,* characterized the transition thus: "The world is thenceforward no God-inspired mystery, but a man-made rationality." The two paintings of St. Francis receiving the stigmata interpret the same subject from two very different points of view: the medieval artist used a "spiritual" vocabulary; the Renaissance one cast the event in worldly terms.

The two paintings opposite, both entitled *St. Francis Receiving the Stigmata,* illustrate how the interpretation of a subject changed during the transition from the Middle Ages to the Renaissance. The work on the left was probably painted about 1235 by Bonaventura Berlinghieri; that on the right is a fresco less than a century later by Giotto or his workshop. Below is *The Nativity,* a painting intended to encourage devotion, by the Renaissance master Piero della Francesca (1420?-1492).

Late in the fourteenth century, the Florentine artist Spinello Aretino was commissioned by a religious order to paint this procession banner, *St. Mary Magdalen with a Crucifix*. It is tempera on canvas.

In subject and form, specific works were sometimes motivated by a particular purpose beyond the broad religious function just described. *Saint Mary Magdalen with a Crucifix* was commissioned of Spinello Aretino around the end of the fourteenth century. Because it was to be carried in religious processions, Aretino painted it in tempera on canvas, a lightweight support; at this early date most paintings not done directly on walls were executed on sturdy wood panels. Raphael's *Madonna di Foligno* had a unique origin. Around 1512, a sizable meteor struck the house of Sigismondo Conti in Foligno. No one was hurt, and Sigismondo commissioned Raphael to paint the altarpiece as a votive offering in gratitude for the lucky escape. The harrowing event is depicted in the background.

The *Madonna di Foligno* (right) by Raphael (1483-1520) was commissioned by Sigismondo Conti as a votive offering, in gratitude that his family escaped injury when a meteorite struck their house. The incident, depicted in the background of the painting, is shown in the detail below.

29

Although for the most part the Greeks did not use art as a means of recording historical events, a famous battle between Alexander the Great and the Persian king Darius III was apparently illustrated in a painting that no longer exists but was the basis for this Pompeiian mosaic. Alexander is seen astride his horse in the fragment on the left; Darius, in his chariot, glares menacingly at him.

ART AS A RECORD

The use of art to chronicle or commemorate historical events has an ancient history. A bas-relief carved around 2500 B.C. shows a Mesopotamian king, Naram-sin, trampling on the bodies of his slain enemies, while others of the defeated army beg for mercy. The bas-reliefs that decorated the royal palace of the Assyrian empire are complete visual records of campaigns from inital savage attack to the slaughter of the defeated and the sacking and burning of their cities.

The Romans recorded notable military events and conquests with the flair and fidelity of modern war correspondents. A gigantic column in Rome, erected by the Emperor Trajan in 114 A.D., records in a continuous spiraling relief the campaigns of Trajan and his legions against the Dacians. Although the column constitutes a blow-by-blow account of the battles of Dacia, it was not primarily intended to instruct, since most of the reliefs are out of visual range, but rather to commemorate the events and impress upon Romans the might of their Emperor.

Throughout the Middle Ages, virtually all events contemporary and historical — in fact, all learning and experience — were interpreted in religious terms. One of the greatest works of art created to record a historical event is the 230-foot-long strip of linen on which were embroidered designs illustrating the Norman Conquest of England in 1066. This tapestry, commissioned about 1080 by Odo, Archbishop of Bayeaux Cathedral, was certainly meant to be read; it was a visual sermon. The message that lay behind the event as it was depicted in the *Bayeaux Tapestry* was unmistakable: by God's will right had triumphed.

Pre-Christian history was seen to prefigure the Christian revelation or to demonstrate the woes that befell the pagan, and to present a moral. A late medieval manuscript, *Lives of Famous Women*, included the story of the rape of Lucretia, which was considered to have caused the overthrow of an early Roman monarchy. Although somewhat on the lurid side, the story was admissible because of what it taught about the high costs of dishonor.

With the Renaissance came a new and secular approach to the world. God remained the undisputed Lord of Creation, but man assumed a new character. He took center stage; he was "the measure of all things." Human experiences, events, and appearances took on a new importance, and, as might be expected, they were translated into painting with increasing frequency. Nearly every great historical moment (and a host of minor incidents) from the Renaissance onwards has been dutifully recorded by some artist or other. The changing attitude toward the world and men's place in it was reflected in the Renaissance paintings, which demonstrated greater and greater "realism." Facility in depicting subjects realistically was gained through painstaking study of space, light and shadow, atmospheric effects, anatomy, proportions, and it was exercised to record man, his activities, and the world around him.

A scene from the melodramatic but moral-bearing story of Lucretia, from a late medieval French manuscript.

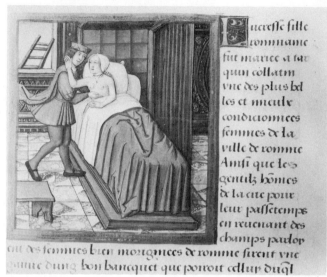

Paolo Uccello (1396-1475) was concerned with the problem of rendering space convincingly (that is, with perspective), as is evident in this panel called *The Battle of San Romano*. It was painted about 1450 to commemorate a victory of Florence over Siena in 1432.

31

Delight in the world and in the works of man, particularly those of classical antiquity, led to such tours de force as *The Interior of the Pantheon,* an eighteenth-century painting by Giovanni Paolo Panini (1691/92-1765).

LANDSCAPE AND STILL LIFE

Delight in the natural world prompted landscape painting of all sorts, from the idylls of Nicolas Poussin and Claude Lorrain and the solemn expanses of Rembrandt, Jacob van Ruisdael, and Hobbema to the sparkling, light-filled scenes captured by Turner, Constable, and the Impressionists. A similar delight in the world and the works of man produced such diverse scenes as the neat, homely interiors by de Hooch and Terborch and grandiose monuments like that in *The Interior of the Pantheon* by Giovanni Paolo Panini.

The emergence of landscape painting and interiors in the seventeenth century was a sign of the increasing popularization of art. A middle class with the affluence to patronize painters was developing. The subject matter demanded by the prosperous burghers focused upon and intensified the delights of the immediate and familiar world. Their enjoyment of material advantages found eloquent expression, too, in still life.

Still-life painting, perhaps more than any other, connotes pleasure in what is "here and now" by simply being what it is — a felicitous arrangement of perishable props (fruit, vegetables, flowers, and the like). And this is its beauty; it is simply what it is and pleasant to look at. It might be left at that, were man not a moralizing as well as a pleasure-seeking creature. Because he is, however, the simple, direct subject matter of the still life was also turned to sermonizing. Perhaps the perishability of the props suggested the theme. Still lifes frequently carried a message about the transitory nature of all things, a reminder of death; hence the names they are variously given — *vanitas vanitatum* and *memento mori*. They are allegories for contemplation. Seventeenth-century painters juxtaposed lush arrangements of flowers or fruit with skulls, while the following century preferred such props as the hourglass, half-consumed candle, withered flower, or, occasionally, a skull resting on a book.

PORTRAITURE

The Renaissance view of man led directly to an impassioned concept of individuality. From the Renaissance onward, man lost the anonymity that characterized him in the Middle Ages and emerged as an increasingly vibrant, interesting, and self-interested being. Art has reflected the development of man's interest in himself every step of the way, from the brilliant anatomical sketches made by Leonardo da Vinci out of a desire to understand man's physical nature to the twentieth-century paintings by Salvador Dali that dissect man's subconscious drives and dreams.

The Renaissance pursuit of individuality had many meanings and followed many avenues. It involved self-awareness and the desire to gain recognition in the eyes of the world, an ambition that could be realized through power, achievement, genius, wealth. Importance was no longer only a matter of birthright; it could be attained by action. Every aspect of a man's life was scrutinized. How he looked, what he did, where he was, what he said and felt, all were of consequence. One reflection of this study of man was the rise of portraiture.

Portraiture was not a Renaissance invention. Actually, its origin is not to be found in painting but in sculpture. The figures carved for tombs by ancient Egyptian sculptors were portraits of a kind: they were generally simplified, but they contained the essential aspects of the individual's appearance. They were not meant to function outside the tomb, however, and they therefore are quite different from modern portraiture.

The forerunners of modern portraiture are found in the sculpture of imperial Rome, particularly the portrait busts. These originated in funerary rites, like the Egyptian portraits. The bust form (i.e., the head, neck, and about as much of the chest and shoulders as would be revealed by a scooped neckline) was determined by the early funerary use of the bust — it was mounted on a frame that was then clothed in the deceased's garments. This lifelike figure was carried in procession and afterward served in private household and ancestor-worship rites. This realism, which initially served the dead, was turned to the service of the living and the state by the time of the Roman Empire. Busts depicted those who gave distinguished service and, of course, the Emperor himself. Thus, the Roman portrait came to be associated with worldly fame and power, a concept which was warmly compatible with Renaissance views of man more than a millennium later.

Portraiture was not unknown in the later Middle Ages. In many altarpieces we can discover an individualized figure who seems to be a devout spectator: he is, in fact, the donor of the altarpiece, who rewarded himself for his deed by having the artist include him in the scene. This convention was continued into the Renaissance. In Raphael's *Madonna di Foligno* (page 29), for example, Sigismondo Conti is seen kneeling on the right. St. Jerome stands behind him with one hand placed upon Sigismondo's head and the other outspread in a reverent gesture toward the Madonna.

Part and parcel of the early development of the Renaissance was the concerted effort to uncover the classical past, and as the forms of Roman art (which included the Greek forms the Romans had borrowed) came to light, they were adopted, copied, and assimilated. Thus, the conventional form of the portait bust,

Portraiture has assumed many forms and has ranged in scale from miniature to monumental. Two examples of miniatures are reproduced here actual size. Top, *Miniature Portrait of a Young Man* in oil and vellum by Hans Holbein (1497?-1543); bottom, the portrait of Hannah Vincent Everett by John Wesley Jarvis (1781?-1839). (The portrait of Mrs. Beardsley reproduced on page 37 shows the sitter wearing such a miniature portrait of her husband on a ribbon around her neck.)

which had expired with the Roman Empire, was faithfully picked up in the fifteenth century and has been imitated without interruption to this day.

As the religious context of the Middle Ages gave way to the secular, portraiture naturally came to be linked with secular matters. A remarkable work, *Jan Arnofini and His Wife,* painted in 1434 by Jan van Eyck, is thought to be a solemn record of a betrothal. It was signed by the artist in a rather unorthodox fashion — *Johannes de eyck fuit hic* ("Jan van Eyck was present"), meaning that the artist was also acting as a witness to the event.

The exchange of portraits frequently preceded important marriage alliances — often arranged without the meeting of the parties involved — and in this respect no artist was kept busier by a single patron than Hans Holbein was by the much-marrying Henry VIII of England. The custom, which initially attended only royal marriages, soon filtered down through the aristocracy to the untitled, and by the nineteenth century it had become widespread in the middle class. The tokens were no longer the harbingers of mighty alliances but evidence of the tender sentiment that marriage betokened. Most of these portraits were miniatures, like the one of Hannah Vincent Everett by John Wesley Jarvis.

It might seem to the layman that all portraits by nature must look pretty much alike except for the different physical characteristics of the sitters, and that portraiture must be comparatively boring for the artist. Nothing could be farther from the truth. Just as each individual is far more than external appearance, so each portrait is more than a painted image. It is a reflection of the sitter, the artist, and their moment in time.

As man took on individuality and importance in his own eyes, he "emerged" in portraits. In the fifteenth century, portraits were largely done in profile (a convention inherited from the donor figures already mentioned). Piero della Francesca painted Federigo da Montefeltro, Duke of Urbino, against a distant, shimmering Italian landscape. He recorded every wart and wrinkle of the massive head, even to the disfigured nose (Federigo lost his right eye and the bridge of his nose in a tournament accident) — a sum of features that should be ugly, even grotesque. Yet it is not. There is an impression of benign, contained force, intelligence, even magnificence. Federigo was one of the great rulers of the Renaissance, a benevolent tyrant uncommonly gifted with intellect, wisdom, and strength, and it is these intangible qualities that the portrait conveys.

The artists of the early Renaissance produced uncompromising records of humanity like this masterly fifteenth-century portrait of Federigo da Montefeltro, Duke of Urbino, by Piero della Francesca.

By the time of Paolo Veronese (1528-1588), the focus of portraiture had widened and painters paid greater heed to surroundings, props, garments, and pose. Veronese's *Portrait of Daniele Barbaro* is dignified and personal.

In the sixteenth century, the figure turned to look out from the canvas. At the same time, the scope of the portrait widened. It took in more of the sitter, showing more of his garments and surroundings, as if to tell more about him. The portrait of Daniele Barbaro by Veronese illustrates the new approach, which was adopted by a host of subsequent portrait painters, including America's first painters, the limners.

The limners, largely anonymous silversmiths, joiners, and sign painters who occasionally turned out a portrait, were for the most part self-taught. Adopting the broad conventions of European portraiture, these craftsmen of the seventeenth and eighteenth century skirted the problem of subtle modeling in light and shadow to create the illusion of three dimensions, since this required great skill and training. In their portraits we find direct, flat, uncompromising images such as that of Mrs. Hezekiah Beardsley. The qualities admirably reflect the limners' sturdy, no-nonsense colonial subjects.

Late Renaissance fashion was to become formula, skillfully perpetuated by academy-trained artists. But the style also prompted vigorous provincial versions like this portrait of Mrs. Hezekiah Beardsley by an unknown American painter of the Connecticut School.

Expressive distortion may produce its own powerful vocabulary, as in the well-known *Guernica*, a fierce indictment of the senseless brutalities of warfare by Pablo Picasso.

A twentieth-century portrait that is a geography of the mind — *The Phantom Landscape (Mountain)* by the surrealist painter, René Magritte (1898-1967).

In this century, the snapshot has taken the place of the painted portrait. Only among the very wealthy or illustrious — heads of church and state, board chairmen, university presidents — is there a demand for the imposing portrait done in the traditional manner. But this is a diminishing demand, and does not reflect our own time or the concerns of the contemporary artist. Artists today don't paint portraits in the fashion of the Renaissance because the image is incongruous. The individual has somehow lost his secure sense of identity in the course of being catapulted into the modern age, and the twentieth-century artist, if he resorts to the human figure at all, is more concerned with the internal dilemmas of modern man than with external likenesses. In *Guernica*, Picasso used fragmented, distorted figures to convey the horrors of bombing and the slaughter of innocents that attend modern warfare. Realism today has been remarkably redirected, as can be seen in René Magritte's portrait with the arcane title *The Phantom Landscape (Mountain)*. The modeling is somewhat softer and more refined, the whole more realistic to our eyes than an early Renaissance portrait, but the result oddly enough leads away from life. Of course, the word "mountain" cutting across the woman's face takes the painting still farther from the traditional function and conventions of the portrait.

Andrew Wyeth, when he uses the figure, re-creates it with a perfect realism that may come from impeccable academic training. Yet his figures, far from affirming humanity, convey poignant desolation and isolation, as may be seen in *Christina's World* (page 108). Other artists have broken down the figure into basic geometric forms, dissolved it into amorphous shapes, or rendered its skeletal or visceral aspect (as in Willem de Kooning's *Women in Landscape IV*). In all, the Renaissance view of man has been replaced as surely as modern man has replaced Renaissance man.

Distortion of the human figure is commonplace in contemporary painting. This denotes not only the artist's freedom to handle subject matter as he wishes but also, more significantly, his pursuit of realities that lie behind surface appearances. This explosive work, *Woman in Landscape IV*, was painted by Willem de Kooning in 1968.

M. KNOEDLER & CO.

In *The Telephone*, the modern painter John Koch depicted a corner of his studio

The studio is the artist's workshop. It may be a disheveled garret like those described by romantic novelists, or a spacious, well-appointed, high-ceilinged room with a skylight or large windows. Ordinarily it is neither of these. For most artists, professionals and amateurs alike, the studio is a modest-sized room (or work area), spacious enough to work in and to accommodate and store equipment and materials.

Having adequate space to work in is a tremendous help to the painter, although not an utter necessity. Joseph Gatto, one of the major (though lesser known) American primitives, lived and worked in a single miniscule dingy room lit by a bare light bulb; his "studio" was one cramped corner where he propped up his canvas on a wooden chair. Yet Gatto painted incessantly for years in spite of these conditions. Needless to say, Gatto's situation was not ideal. It would discourage most people from the very notion of painting in the first place. The work area, although it can offer no guarantees, should at least nurture creativity, not stifle it. Anyone who is going to do any painting at all should look about for the best possible place; hopefully it will far surpass what Gatto had to put up with.

SELECTING THE SPACE

The studio need not be vast; it is more important that it be well organized, properly lighted, and at least relatively comfortable and quiet. An area as small as eight by twelve feet could conceivably serve if it were planned for maximum use of the space; an area twice the size would serve infinitely better. But size is a matter of individual preference and circumstances.

Where the studio is located may be even more important than its size. Since it is to be a work area, it should be separate from — not in the middle of — whatever else may be going on. For example, it should not be a room used frequently for other distracting activities (such as watching television) or an area that is also a thoroughfare. Ideally, the studio should be a space that is truly set aside and furthermore left undisturbed between painting sessions.

2.
The Studio

THE "OFF LIMITS" RULE

The studio should, at least in principle, be "off limits" to everyone — including spouses with the compulsion to tidy up, curious friends and neighbors, and children. These are two important reasons for this. One is that damage may unwittingly be done to the work itself and consequently to the artist's morale. An unfixed pastel or charcoal sketch or a wet painting may be ruined just by brushing against it, to say nothing of what will come of its being shuffled about. No one but the artist can be expected to know precisely where — or how much — caution should be exercised. A scrap of paper may beckon to be thrown in the wastebasket or used for the grocery list; that it contains a sketch or notation that is of value to the artist is not always apparent. Thus, most artists protect their work area with a ferocity that is utterly baffling to everyone around them — baffling, that is, to everyone but other artists.

The second reason that the studio should be off limits, *especially to children*, has to do with the nature of the artist's tools and materials. Some of them are lethal,

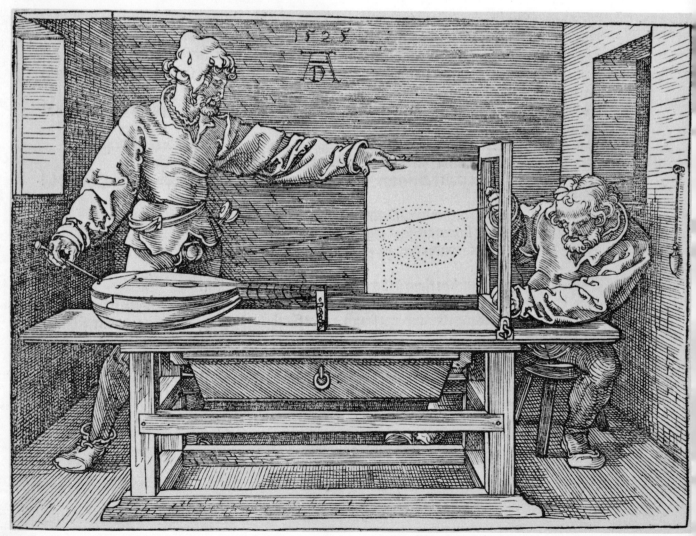

Artists at work through the centuries. Opposite, top, a medieval craftsman illuminates a manuscript while another paints a panel. From the pattern book of Reun Monastery, about 1200. Bottom, the use of a perspective device to draw a lute, a sixteenth-century print by Albrecht Dürer (1471-1528). At right, Dürer's contemporary, Lancelot Blondeel, depicted an artist as St. Luke painting the Virgin. Below, *The Painters' Triumph* by the nineteenth-century American genre painter, William Sydney Mount.

The work of two true primitive painters. Above *Washington Square* by Joseph Gatto; left, *Moon Landing* by Frank Cicero.

and it is not readily clear which are and which are not. It is obvious that mat knives are razor-sharp. It is not so obvious (particularly to a child) that some pigments are extremely poisonous and that some solvents are highly flammable or give off toxic vapors — or both. Such materials should also be kept well out of reach just as in a woodworking shop dangerous tools such as power saws are stored with particular care.

LIGHT AND VENTILATION

In selecting a place to paint, both lighting and ventilation should be taken into account. A great deal of indirect sunlight is ideal, and a room with large windows facing north will provide this. (North light is preferable because it is the most constant.) But if direct sunlight streams through a window (or windows), it is not a serious drawback. The light can be diffused by putting something over the glass — for example, rice paper glued to the panes or thin, gauzelike material stretched

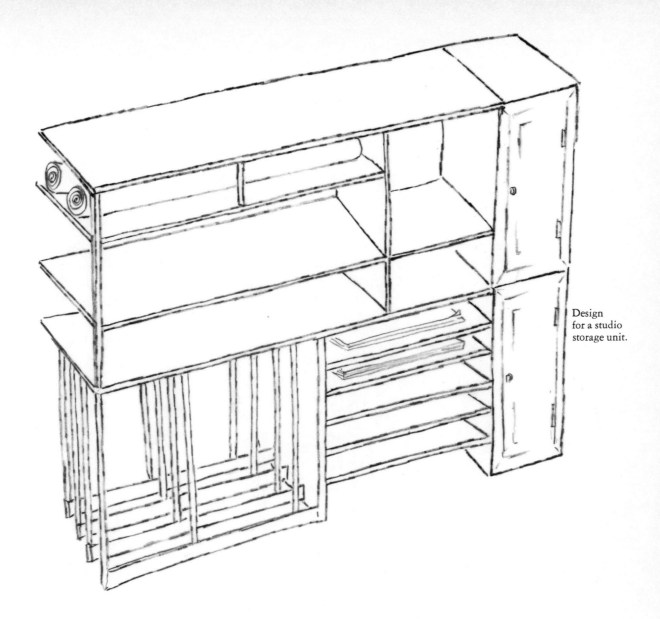

STUDIO FURNITURE

over the window and lightly tacked to the window frame.

All work on a painting should be done under the same lighting conditions, and to ensure this it is best not to mix natural and artificial light. If you must work with artificial light, a simple ceiling fixture probably will be adequate. Select the light bulbs or fluorescent tubes with care, however. Ordinary light bulbs have distinctly warm overtones; many fluorescent tubes produce equally exaggerated cool blue light. There are both light bulbs and fluorescent tubes that more or less closely approximate "natural" light (i.e., daylight), and these should be used in the studio.

The work area must also be adequately ventilated by some means or other. "Adequate" does not mean simply the minimum for working comfort; at times, when volatile solvents are used, for example, there should be a generous amount of well-circulating fresh air. Especially in a small space, a window that can be opened wide is essential.

Very little furniture is needed to make a well-appointed studio: a chair, a sturdy table, some shelves, and, perhaps, a cabinet are the basics. The expense involved need not be great; if you must buy any of these items, you can obtain them secondhand for very little.

If you install shelves specifically for art materials, you might plan them as shown in the accompanying sketch. This plan incorporates elements that will answer most storage needs. For example, there is a long shelf at about eye level for rolls of canvas and long stretcher bars. Several shallow shelves on the right below are for stacks of paper, mat board, and the like. On the left below, the space is divided by vertical bars attached to lightweight runners on the floor. This racklike arrangement is very useful for storing paintings, particularly if several are in progress at one time and are therefore still wet or unfixed.

EQUIPMENT

The piece of equipment most closely associated with the artist's studio is the easel. Essentially it is a stand made to hold a painting, and it may be as simple as the one depicted in *The Painter's Triumph* (reproduced on page 43) — a three-legged type with the back leg hinged and pegs to hold the painting. More complicated easels have two upright posts on a base with wheels or casters, a narrow adjustable shelf on which to rest the painting, a mechanism to adjust the tilt of the painting, etc. The line drawings show three types of easels, including one specifically designed for watercolor work (the two small drawings on the right); here the painting surface may be adjusted from a vertical to a horizontal position.

Traditionally, easels are made of wood, although now they are also manufactured in aluminum. The sketches on the left and in the center show two types of wooden studio easels — the elaborate kind mentioned previously and a more modest version that is perfectly suitable.

Lightweight easels that can be folded down into an easily portable package were developed about a century ago when landscape painters, in pursuit of naturalism, took to the out-of-doors to work. The portable easel, camp stool, and compact paint box designed to carry palette, paints, and brushes are still standard equipment for work away from the studio. In the studio the somewhat heavier, sturdier easel is generally more satisfactory.

Three types of easel.

SABLE WATERCOLOR BRUSHES

14

9

4

OVAL WASH BRUSH

½

¾"

1"

FAN BRUSH

2

A variety of soft hair brushes.

The painter's most essential tool is, of course, the brush. Brushes have not changed greatly throughout the history of painting because their function — that of applying and spreading paint — has remained the same. They consist now, as always, of tufts of hair or fiber attached to some sort of handle (although the ancient Egyptians also used a simpler version — a reed, whose fibers were steeped and separated at one end to form the brush).

By the time of classical Greece and Rome, the two

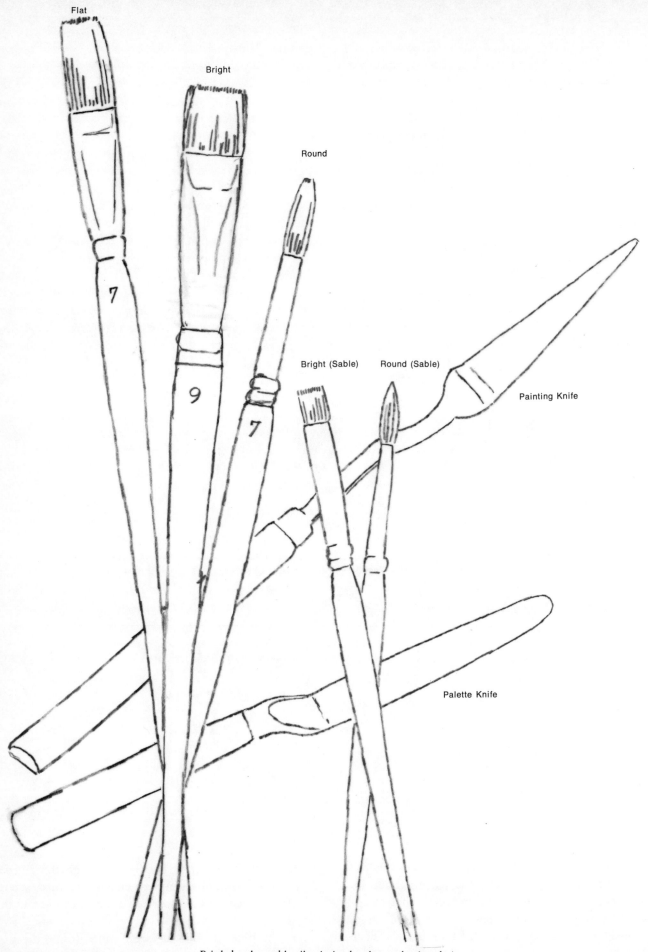

Flat

Bright

Round

Bright (Sable)   Round (Sable)

Painting Knife

Palette Knife

7

9

7

Bristle brushes, sable oil-painting brushes, and palette knives.

kinds of brush we use now apparently had evolved. These are hard bristle brushes, made from hog's or boar's bristles, and soft hair brushes. Fine hair brushes are sable, and the finest are made from Russian red sable, using only the hair of the tail. Other soft hair brushes are called camel, although they are never made from camel hair but rather, most frequently, from squirrel.

The range of brush materials, shapes, and specialized uses has always been greater in the East than in the West. The Chinese and Japanese made brushes from the hair of the deer, goat, rabbit, wolf, and other animals, from human hair, and even from feathers; the handles, although normally of bamboo, were also made of bone, silver, or ivory. A strict tradition prescribed what kind of brush was to be used for specific lines or subjects.

The one significant innovation in the making of brushes occurred in the nineteenth century, when metal ferrules to hold the brush to the handle were introduced. Until then, brushes had always been round; the metal ferrule made possible the flat brush.

Brushes today are of three main types: flat, bright, and round. The flat has a ferrule that is flat at the brush end, and the bristles are of an even length. The bright is similar to the flat, but with shorter bristles (or hair). The round is set in a round ferrule, and the hairs or bristles are gathered so that they taper toward the tip.

Brushes should be selected with care — especially sables, which are expensive. Always test them before buying them. Ask for a container of water and immerse the ones you are considering. A good brush comes to a perfect point when withdrawn from the water. Be sure that the curve of the brush in silhouette from the ferrule to the tip is smoothly convex all around, with no unevenness, dips, or concavities. Finally, bend the brush over. It should spring back when the pressure is removed. A poor brush lacks resiliency and will remain bent.

Another basic tool of the painter is the knife, which may be used for a variety of purposes. There are two main types. The painting knife is very flexible and tapers sharply toward the end; there are a number of sizes and variations on the basic shape. The other type, the palette knife, is less flexible and has a broad blade with a rounded end. It is used primarily for mixing pigments and scraping paint off the palette, but it is also used to spread paint onto the support.

The drawing board is an extremely useful piece of equipment. Drawing boards are manufactured specifically for the artist's use, and they come in many sizes from 12 by 17 inches to 31 by 42 inches. If you have but one, a medium-large size (about 18 by 24 inches) probably is the best choice.

By no means a necessity, but very handy, is a large bulletin board (or simply a generous piece of soft wallboard) affixed to a wall near where you work. On it, sketches and notations can be tacked up and referred to at a glance.

The easel, drawing board, and bulletin board will be useful no matter what medium you choose. The assortment of brushes you need will depend upon the medium; in addition, special equipment may be required by a particular medium. Such equipment, which could range in complexity and cost from a twenty-five-cent atomizer for fixing pastels to a relatively costly heated palette for encaustic work, will be taken up as the individual media are discussed.

Portrait of a Lady with an Ostrich-Feather Fan by Rembrandt. Oil on canvas.

The following seven chapters are devoted to the "traditional" media — watercolor (including gouache and distemper), casein, fresco, encaustic, tempera, oils, and pastels. They appear in this order because, if conjecture may be allowed, this may have been the order in which they made their historical appearance.

Actually, the beginnings of all the more ancient media are quite obscure. We cannot be certain that the earliest extant examples of a medium represent the earliest practice; in fact, we may be assured they do not. Encaustic was practiced for centuries prior to the Fayum portraits; fresco undoubtedly evolved over a long period before the examples at Knossos were painted, and so on.) The precise techniques employed are equally elusive, and thus the best efforts to reconstruct early methods and materials are also somewhat conjectural. The unanswered questions are legion.

It would be a mistake, however, to assume that there is — or should be — a single, absolute, and authoritative way to use any medium. Each has encompassed a variety of materials and methods, serving different needs at the same or different times. The media themselves certainly were never sacrosanct. They were used so long as they were useful, abandoned when others would serve better, and revived only when their qualities were once again in demand. At least such has been the case until recently. Now a passion for history and an awareness of the art of all the ages have prompted a pursuit of media per se. Which is fine, so long as the tail doesn't wag the dog. Having something to express is the foremost consideration; selecting the most suitable way to express it follows.

TRADITIONAL MEDIA

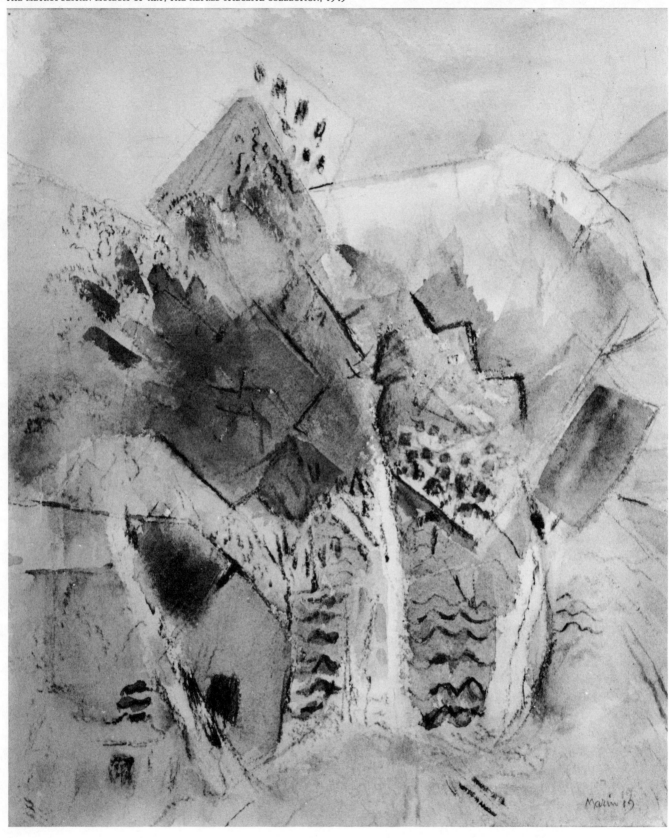

The ancient and highly flexible watercolor medium has been used with great verve by many twentieth-century artists. Illustrated is *Tree Forms, Stonington, Maine* by John Marin (1870-1953). A charcoal underdrawing has been incorporated into the composition.

INTRODUCING WATERCOLOR

A precise distinction is now drawn between transparent watercolor, sometimes called aquarelle, the opaque version called gouache, and the variation, related to gouache, called distemper. Although all are by definition watercolor — that is, they are pigments dissolved in water — they have individual characteristics and qualities that make it convenient to discuss them separately. The first part of this chapter deals with transparent watercolor, which will be referred to here simply as watercolor.

The use of water-based pigments is probably as old as painting itself. In terms of its physical makeup, watercolor is, in a sense, the most basic, least sophisticated medium. It consists only of ground pigments mixed with a simple binder such as vegetable gum or animal glue and dissolved in water, which is the vehicle. When the paint has been applied, the water evaporates, leaving the pigment and the binder, which holds it to the support.

The earliest extant watercolors are the wall and panel paintings (and later papyrus paintings) of ancient Egypt. These date from the beginning of the third millennium B.C., nearly five thousand years ago. The same medium was used by the Greeks and Romans, and, subsequently, by medieval artists.

Between the late Middle Ages and the early Renaissance, egg tempera and then oils began to supplant watercolor as a major medium, and from the fifteenth to the eighteenth century watercolor was used primarily for sketches. Among the finest examples of these are the sparkling, meticulous visual notes Albrecht Dürer made of his travels. Throughout this period, however, watercolor remained in use; it was the favored medium of the miniaturists, who emerged during the sixteenth century. The earliest of the great miniaturists, the Eng-

3.
Watercolor

eius uel corporali uel spuali
necessitate subleuanda: De-
uotius operare;
Dominica VIIII POST OCT PEN.
Lc sci eu. scdm matheu.
Nimo K. Dixit ihc dis
cipulis suis; Nemo potest
duobus dominis seruire;
Et cetera; Omel vener bede
pbri. de eade. lix.
Nemo
potest
duob;
domini
seruire:
quia n
ualet
simul transi_
toria
na
& eter
diligere; Si
eternitate dili
Cuncta teporalia
in usu Hon in affectu

Pigments with a simple vegetable-gum or animal-glue binder were used in medieval manuscript illuminations like the one at the left from an eleventh-century French cathedral lectionary. Below is one of the earliest portrait miniatures, painted about 1590 by Nicholas Hilliard. Since white pigment was used in the paint, the medium is the version of watercolor now called gouache.

lishman Nicholas Hilliard, a favorite of Queen Elizabeth, used transparent colors along with colors mixed with white, which is to say he combined watercolor with gouache.

The nineteenth century saw the full restoration of watercolor to a position of first-rank importance. In the watercolors of J. M. W. Turner and Winslow Homer, the medium reached a zenith: their delicate washes and spare strokes evoke whole scenes bathed in sun or shimmering in luminous mists. In the twentieth century, the medium has served the diverse expressions of such artists as Raoul Dufy, Paul Klee, John Marin, and Andrew Wyeth.

In *Hurricane, Bahamas* (above) by Winslow Homer (1836-1910), the forms are suggested by controlled transparent washes and summary brushwork. Below is *The First Hepaticas* by Charles Burchfield (1893-1967), a watercolor of an eerie primeval forest.

One advantage of watercolor painting is that it requires a minimum of materials and equipment — paints and paper, a palette, a few brushes, and a container of water. The paints can be purchased either in tubes or small pans. Traditionally, and before the advent of tubes, the pigments were prepared in small dry cakes, and they can be obtained in this form or in powdered form from the larger art suppliers. However, most artists prefer the tubes.

PALETTE

The term "palette" has two meanings. In its most familiar sense, it refers to the board or other surface on which an artist lays his pigments and mixes his paint. The palette of a particular painting medium, however, refers to the list or set of pigments that can be used with the medium; not all pigments can be used with all media.

Although a great range of pigments is available for painting in watercolor, the most permanent ones are preferable for obvious reasons. These include such families of pigments as cadmium (yellow, orange, and red), Mars (yellow, orange, red, violet, brown, and black), cobalt (yellow, blue, and violet), manganese (blue and violet), alizarin (red, violet, and brown), phthalocyanine (blue and green), and the raw and burnt siennas and umbers, and such individual pigments as strontium yellow, barium yellow, ultramarine blue, cerulean blue, chromium-oxide green, green earth, lampblack, and ivory black.

SUPPORTS

The most common support for watercolor is good-quality rag paper. Numerous varieties are manufactured with the characteristics of watercolor expressly in mind: they are made with chemicals that will not adversely affect the pigments and with appropriate size (the substance used to coat and fill the surface) in carefully regulated amounts, and they are produced by a rolling and pressing method that creates an open-textured surface and uniform, regular grain. Watercolor paper is white and comes in a number of sizes, weights (or thicknesses), and surface textures, from coarse to very fine. As with most art supplies, the papers range greatly in price and quality; the finest always carry the watermark of the manufacturer — Strathmore, Fabriano, Whatman, etc. — in the corner of each sheet and are more costly.

The thin, lighter-weight papers generally must be stretched on a drawing board or mounted on a permanent backing before painting begins; otherwise, as the colors are applied, the water will cause the paper to wrinkle and become increasingly limp. You can stretch a sheet of paper by immersing it in water or sponging both sides and affixing it to a drawing board with brown-paper (butcher's) tape. The paper will shrink and pull taut as it dries. All but the heaviest watercolor paper should be stretched and mounted in this way if the painting is going to require much working over. Rapid sketches or preliminary studies, on the other hand, may be done on watercolor pads or small, unmounted sheets tacked to a drawing board.

Although paper is the most common support for watercolor, it is not the only one possible. Paper did not make its appearance in the West until sometime in the thirteenth century, and watercolor painting was practiced for many thousands of years before that. Although most of the supports used historically are no longer practicable for general purposes, some of them are still available and may be mentioned for their special qualities.

The earliest watercolors still extant are the Egyptian paintings mentioned before; most of them were done on tomb and temple walls. These were variously prepared, often covered with a foundation of straw-reinforced mud "plaster" and overlaid with a thin layer of stucco.

The use of wood panels as supports is generally associated with the Middle Ages, but if we may judge by what has survived, here too the Egyptians were the originators. A remarkable painting called the *Geese of Meidum*, which dates from the Fourth Dynasty (2900–2750 B.C.), was done on a panel that was prepared with a light whitewash.

Some of the earliest medieval manuscripts were executed on papyrus, a material (made from the inner membranes of the stalks of the papyrus plant) inherited from the Egyptians. By far the most common support used during the Middle Ages, however, was parchment; it is the material of the magnificent illuminated manuscripts. Parchment is made from the skin of an animal, usually goat, sheep, or cow, that is soaked in a water and lime solution, stretched on a frame, and scraped smooth. (Vellum is properly a fine-grained parchment made from lambskin, kidskin, or calfskin.) Today, there are a number of products called parchment paper, calligraphic vellum, etc., which are paper, not genuine parchment; but genuine parchment is available at any large art supplier.

To such historically widely used supports as parchment, wood panels, and walls must be added textiles. Here again, we can trace the use of the support back to Egypt. In the inner coffins of the end of the Late Kingdom (c. 525 B.C.), stucco-soaked swathing cloths served

Region of Brooklyn Bridge Fantasy by John Marin, one of the foremost twentieth-century watercolorists.

Bare Willows and Distant Landscape by Ma Yüan, a Chinese landscape artist of the Sung Dynasty (960-1279). The demanding technique combine succint brushstrokes and washes for tonal gradations.

as a cocoon-like encasement for the dead. Facial features and funerary symbols and signs were elaborately painted on the hardened shell. In essence, this is a version of the most familiar modern support — sized linen — today used for oil paintings. Now, of course, it is usually sized and stretched on a frame, rather than being stiffened in the way the Egyptians prepared it, and it is only rarely used as a support for watercolor.

For the most significant, continuous, and eloquent use of a textile support with watercolor we must look to th East. Paper is said to have been invented in China, ye even after its appearance silk was generally considere more worthy for paintings. The long history of Chines painting unfolds with two constants — the watercol medium and the silk support, the silk mounted on pape to make it more firm. (The highly absorbent Chines paper was occasionally used as a support but never com pletely superseded silk.) Painting on silk required a

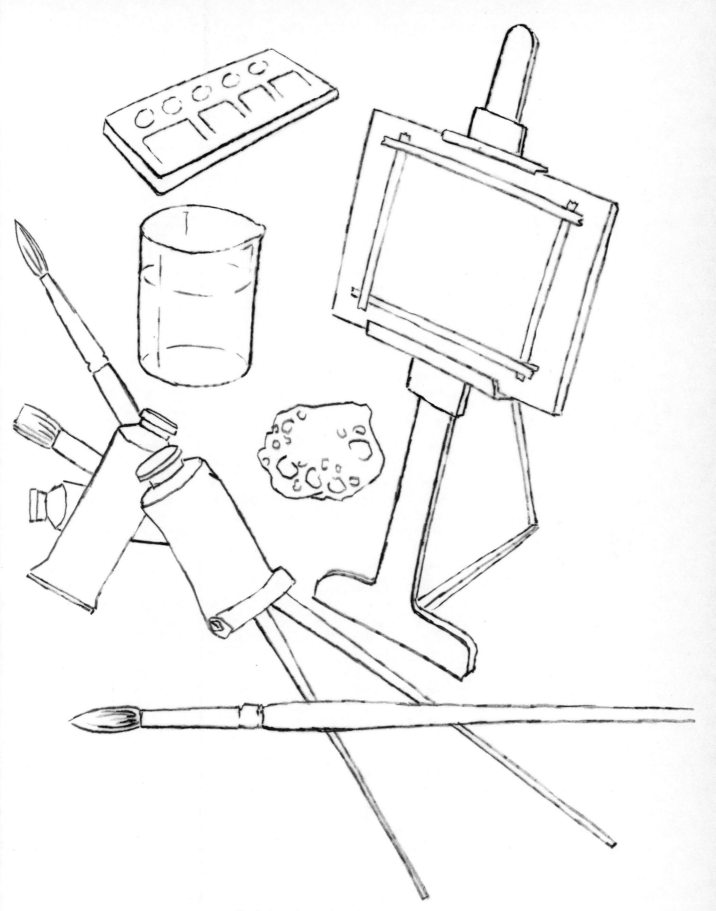

The basic equipment for painting in watercolor.

exceptionally steady hand capable of capturing in a few strokes the image in the artist's mind. The tradition and the materials themselves allowed for no corrections. This demanding technique arose from a meditative and spiritual attitude toward painting. The first canon or law of Chinese painting, formulated by Hsieh-Ho in the sixth century, says that painting shall discover the rhythmic vitality or spiritual rhythm expressed in the movement of life. The Chinese artist was not principally concerned with the surface appearance of things (as has been the case in much European art), but with their essence. Through meditation he sought to unite with that essence or life force and then to express it. His materials and techniques were perfectly suited to his purpose. Those employed in Western art would not have contained this kind of expression so well, for they were evolved to suit a more outward, materialistic tradition.

Silk has also been used for watercolor in the West. Early in the Christian era the silk industry spread from China, and by the thirteenth century sericulture was practiced in Italy and France and silk became increasingly available in Europe. Since then, although never widely used as a support, it has been in continual, if occasional use. Two rather unusual examples may be mentioned. One is the *Paremont de Norbonne*, an altar frontal painted on silk in monochromatic watercolors for Charles V, Holy Roman Emperor. The other — decorated fans — occurred in the eighteenth and early nineteenth centuries, when *chinoiserie* became fashionable. Superficial encounters with Eastern cultures caught the fancy of a Europe somewhat flagging in vitality and imagination, and the result was a rash of Chinese-style ornaments, furniture, and other items, including the silk fans painted in watercolor with Oriental motifs.

BRUSHES AND OTHER EQUIPMENT

To have a few good brushes is of the greatest importance in watercolor painting. The brushes are usually those made of soft hair rather than stiff bristles. Two or three fine sables are all you need. Sizes range from #000 to #14; a good assortment might include three rounds: one small size (#3 or #4), one medium (#9), and one large (#12 or #14). To these basic tools might be added a flat brush ¾ inch to 1 inch wide. A good #3 or #4 round will come to a perfect point, so that using just the tip you can paint the finest details as well as with a #000. The drawing on page 47 shows several rounds and flat brushes of various sizes.

Since fine sable brushes are both essential and relatively costly, they must be cared for properly. After each use wash them with warm water and a mild soap. Then rinse them in warm running water to remove every trace of soap. They should assume perfect points and dry in this position. Stand them brush-end up in a holder of some sort — it may be simply a jar, or any of the more or less elaborate brush holders manufactured for the purpose. If they are to be stored for a long time, put them in a box with a few moth balls and be careful to keep the brush ends from jamming against the end of the box.

You will also need a palette. The type generally used for watercolors is made of white porcelain or white plastic, with depressions for the colors and one or more areas set off for mixing them. A container of water for cleaning brushes and thinning paint is also needed.

AN APPROACH TO PAINTING WITH WATERCOLOR

Watercolors are often the first paints given to children, mainly because they require a minimum of equipment, make less of a mess than other media, and are the easiest to clean up. In spite of the fact that watercolor is perhaps the most difficult medium to master, children use it with astonishing success. Lacking the self-consciousness and caution of adults, they paint the way they speak — simply, directly, and with finality. They are not concerned with grammar or syntax, style or technique, but with what they have to say. This enviable directness is a prime requirement for painting in watercolor. Once a stroke is made, it is final. Reworking is out, for it muddles the pigment into uneven patches. Therefore, knowing ahead of time what effect is desired and precisely what brushwork will achieve it becomes extremely important. What is called for is a calculated, much-rehearsed nonchalance.

One way to achieve the necessary directness is to practice how to control the brushes. Brushwork, the heart of watercolor painting, is determined by the support (its texture, whether it is used dry or wet), the type of brush, the amount of paint and water with which the brush is loaded, and the way the brush is held and manipulated. Various combinations yield a vast number of expressive effects, and one of the greatest delights the medium of watercolor holds is discovering and mastering these effects.

Try these exercises for a start: On dry paper make a number of thin strokes with a pointed brush; then try dabbing and flicking with the brush hairs splayed. Use a flat brush to experiment with heavy, firm strokes; then try chisel-edge strokes and scrubbing with the hairs splayed. Vary the paint and water load of the brush. Try all the same strokes on a wet ground. Try using a

Piazza di San Marco, by Maurice Prendergast (1859-1924), was done completely in transparent watercolor.

flat brush loaded with two or three colors on the wet ground. Take a large, well-loaded round and make a firm stroke; then rinse the brush, shake or blot out the excess water, and run the brush along the edge of the stroke.

These are only a few of the endless brushwork possibilities. Try whatever occurs to you, and when the effect is one that you like, practice it over and over again until you can produce it with ease and sureness.

The way you hold the brush — either as you would hold a pencil or underhand (with the handle almost parallel to the paper) — further controls the effects. Brushes have a balance point: near the ferrule, where the handle is the thickest. They are generally held at this point, but holding them elsewhere increases the range of brushwork. For instance, scrubbing is particularly successful when the brush is held underhand near the ferrule. For flicking and wispy strokes, the brush may be held at the very end of the handle. When the brush is held almost perpendicular to the paper, the tip delivers the paint in delicate lines; held underhand, the entire length of the brush from heel to tip delivers a bold band of pigment that is heavier at the heel side where the brush is thickest and carries the most paint.

Although the medium of watercolor is very old, the modern method of handling it has a relatively brief history. One of the best ways to learn the possibilities of the medium, perhaps, is to follow step by step its evolution, beginning with the techniques of the early "modern" watercolorists, among them Canaletto, Francis Nicholson, and J. S. Cotman, who worked in the late eighteenth and nineteenth century. To approach watercolor as they did, you will create monochrome paintings by using a number of washes of a single color. The virtue of this approach is that you gain control over the brushwork and building up of forms without the added complication of coping with a whole range of colors.

First, lay in the main forms with a light wash. (In a wash, the paint is generously diluted with water.) Remember, you must leave the paper untouched where you want highlights or sparkling whites in the finished painting.

After you have applied the first wash, pick up the darker tones and details with increasingly darker washes. Work "into" the painting — into the deepest recesses, tones, and shadows. Allow each wash to dry before introducing the next.

It is difficult to keep clear the areas that are to remain unpainted, especially at first. If you have painted over an area by mistake, most of the color can be removed by dampening it with a clean, water-laden brush and then, with the brush blotted free of the moisture, pick-

ing up the color. This does not remove every trace of color, and it produces soft edges, but it is a good technique to use if the area to be lightened is large. Another method can be employed if the paper is heavy and of good quality. When the paint is thoroughly dry, scrape it down where you want highlights. This is not practical for large areas, but it does bring out the white sparkle of the paper and gives clean, crisp edges.

From the early watercolorists we can learn yet another way to achieve highlights — by avoiding mistakes in the first place. They simply covered areas to be kept free of paint with a waterproof material that could be removed when the painting was completed. You can do this easily with masking tape.

After you have painted enough monochrome watercolors to feel at ease, the next step is to introduce washes and details of a second color. Now you will discover how washes of different tonal qualities affect each other — how one will advance, another recede — and what effects can be achieved by covering one with another. If your initial wash is a cool tone such as gray or blue, try introducing a warm color in foreground areas and note how forms evolve.

When you have achieved satisfactory results with two washes, lay in washes of several different colors over a monochrome underpainting; that is, add local color — green to trees and shrubbery, reds or browns to buildings, blues to sky or water. This is not to be confused with the coloring in of outlined areas in a finished drawing, which is a technique based on different principles, with qualities of its own. In it, color is an adjunct to the drawing. Watercolor used in this way is not considered painting but rather drawing; it is sometimes referred to as colored drawing or rendering.

The approach suggested above is based on using the initial monochrome wash. When you have developed facility with it, you may begin to substitute color washes applied directly to various areas of the painting. Having practiced brushwork and the use of washes, you will already know many of the effects that can be achieved. From this point on, the direction you take is up to you. Your work can become increasingly free and at the same time increasingly sure. You may use a few brushstrokes, a few colors, and leave much of the paper untouched, like Cézanne, whose watercolors are a marvel of organized forethought and structure. Or you may spread a few bold washes and finish with detailing brushwork, like Winslow Homer. This is not to suggest that you should adopt the style of a great watercolorist but rather to point out that through such practice and experimentation with the diverse expressive possibilities of watercolor you will learn to control the medium and therefore to use it in your own distinctive way.

GOUACHE

INTRODUCING GOUACHE

Gouache is watercolor that has been rendered opaque by the addition of white to the pigments. The degree of opacity varies depending upon the amount of white added.

Opaque and transparent watercolor go hand-in-hand through most of the long history of watercolor. Frequently, both were used in the same painting — as they may be still. The combination is found in the magnificent fifteenth- and sixteenth-century ink drawings by Albrecht Dürer, Peter Vischer the Younger, Hans Holbein the Younger, Wolf Huber, and other masters. Their drawings were created as book illustrations, as studies for paintings, sculpture, or architecture, as preliminary sketches for designs to be wrought on jewelry, armor, or windows, and as sketches for the staging of pageants and processions. In 1650, the English writer Edward Norgate noted in his *Miniatura, or the Art of Limning*, "White is ever a dayly guest, and seldom absent but in the shadowes."

The clear-cut differentiation between opaque and transparent watercolor came about between the late eighteenth and early nineteenth centuries, when a formula was evolved for the use of the transparent medium. The terms "aquarelle" and "gouache" are likewise recent. As defined today, gouache differs greatly from transparent watercolor in both application and effect.

Gouache paintings do not exhibit the sparkling luminosity and clear intensity of color that characterize the transparent medium, and their tonality is generally more subdued, rather reminiscent of pastels.

Gouache is highly flexible, permitting a wide range of expressive uses: the broad, simple areas of Toulouse-Lautrec's *Monsieur Boileau at the Café* (overleaf) and the delicate elaboration of the Indian miniature were both created with gouache. The medium is easier to handle than watercolor or even oil paint. By using different amounts of white and water with the pigments, varying degrees of intensity can be achieved, and the opacity of gouache makes it possible not only to repaint or correct faulty areas, but also to create a variety of effects by overpainting. Like watercolor, gouache dries rapidly, but the resulting surface is different. Watercolor is applied in such a thin film that the texture of the support is essentially unchanged. Gouache, in contrast, can be built up with successive applications or used quite thick initially, almost like oils.

PALETTE

The permanent colors used in gouache painting are the same as those listed for transparent watercolor (page 56), plus Chinese white (the name for zinc white that has been prepared specifically for watercolor use) and titanium white. It is not necessary to have all the colors

Raoul Dufy (1877-1953) combined transparent washes and gouache in this brisk calligraphic impression of *Longchamps Race Track*. The preliminary pencil sketch is a visible, integral part of the painting.

Above, *Prince Riding an Elephant* by Khemka-ran. This album leaf was illustrated in gouache, the preferred medium of Eastern miniaturists, by an artist of the Indian Mughal School, a style that flourished in the late sixteenth century. At right, a gouache, *Monsieur Boileau at the Cafe*, by Henri de Toulouse-Lautrec (1864-1901).

that are available. At first, eight or ten are sufficient: in addition to a white and a black, the following might be selected: cadmium red and yellow, ultramarine blue, viridian or phthalocyanine green, yellow ocher, burnt sienna, and raw umber. Later, the palette may be expanded to include sixteen or eighteen colors.

SUPPORTS

Gouache paintings may be done on a variety of supports, from paper to panel. If you use watercolor paper, stretch it on a drawing board as described in the section on watercolor (page 56). Illustration board also makes a very satisfactory support; just tack it to the drawing board. Some artists use gesso panels (see page 71), and colored grounds and papers are also good supports.

BRUSHES AND OTHER EQUIPMENT

The same brushes used for transparent watercolor — fine sables — are used for gouache, and the colors are laid out on the same kind of palette. Containers of water for cleaning brushes and thinning paint are also needed.

AN APPROACH TO PAINTING WITH GOUACHE

Because gouache is such a versatile medium, there are any number of ways to approach it. Underdrawings may be used, and unlike transparent watercolor, the sketch need not be a part of the finished work: it may be covered over with broad areas of color and developed and refined in any direction.

A good way to begin is to lay in one or two colors, well thinned with water, on a loose drawing. Before the paint has dried completely, you may overpaint it either with more thinned color or with opaque color. The effect, although opaque, will be one of richness and depth. With white, either applied in quite diluted form or thickly scumbled over strong, opaque colors, you can produce an amazing range of light tones. Further overpainting or scumbling (scrubbing a lighter color over a darker one) will heighten the colors and build up darker and lighter tones. Often, in fact, a richer, more distinct color may be achieved by overpainting, scumbling, cross-hatching, and applying washes than by trying to mix the color on the palette. For example, a gray painted over an ocher wash will yield a gray with warm overtones, whereas mixing ocher and gray on the palette will produce a muddy gray.

The texture of a gouache painting is that of the paint itself. You can exploit this inherent quality of the medium by using generous quantities of paint and broad brushwork to build up a slight impasto surface. The impasto cannot be so pronounced as with oils, however. If the paint is piled on too thick, it will crack and fall off.

Gouache dries to a dull matte finish, and most artists prefer to leave it this way. If you wish, however, you can obtain a glazed surface. One method is to varnish the painting using dammar varnish (one part diluted with about two parts turpentine); this will heighten the colors and intensify the blacks, creating an effect similar to that of oils. The medium may also be combined with pastels, inks, oils, pencil, and even crayon.

DISTEMPER

Distemper is a water-base medium that uses the same palette as watercolor and generally contains, like gouache, an opaque filler — a chalk substance. It is differentiated from watercolor and gouache by its binder. Distemper is a size paint, which means the binder is a glue — usually rabbit-skin glue — rather than gum, as in watercolor and gouache.

Distemper has a history of its own. Size was the binder normally employed for watercolor in the Far East. The medium was used for painting panels, illuminating books, and wall painting in India, and it was also employed in China and Japan. According to Pliny, the first-century Roman scholar, classical Greek and Roman painters used glue as well as other binders, including gum and egg. Distemper was frequently employed in wall painting in northern Europe during the Middle Ages and early Renaissance and served, along with gouache and tempera, as a medium for retouching frescoes. A variation of distemper, in which the white of an egg was used with the gum and pigments, was described by the fifteenth-century painter Cennino Cennini, who wrote a handbook for artists. This version of distemper was used again in the nineteenth century by the Swiss landscape painter, Arnold Böcklin.

At the turn of this century, distemper paintings of great delicacy were done by the Impressionist Pierre Bonnard. But the medium has never had widespread general use — it is best known for specific applications. It has long been used for painting such large-scale decorations as theatrical scenery — a practice that may have evolved from its use in painting processional banners and backdrops for Renaissance pageants. The medium is also the basis of the familiar poster paints or showcard colors, which are used by commercial artists not only for posters but for a great variety of purposes.

Chairs, by Russell Woody, a contemporary artist, was painted in casein and subsequently varnished with a synthetic medium.

INTRODUCING CASEIN

o long ago that it is not recorded, someone made the
ather astonishing discovery that a durable cement can
e made from cheese. This is casein cement — or glue
— and it has been used by cabinetmakers from at least
he time of ancient Egypt to the present. It has appar-
ntly been employed as a binder for pigment for nearly
s long: ancient Hebrew writings mention the use of
urd in house painting and decoration. Its parallel mod-
rn use is as the binder for cold-water house paints.

The method of preparing casein has changed little
rom its earliest use. A number of recipes are recorded,
he one by Theophilus in a twelfth-century manuscript
ntitled *Schedula diversarum artium* being representa-
ve: "Take soft cheese, cut it into bits; pound and wash
in a mortar with hot water till all the soluble parts
re removed, and till the water, which requires to be
equently changed, remains clear. The cheese, thus pre-
ared, will crumble like bread when dry, and may be
ept in that state for any length of time. The substance
self is not soluble in water, but it becomes so by the
ddition of quicklime: on pounding it with this a viscous
eam is formed, which may be thinned with water. It
ries quickly, and once dry cannot be again dissolved."

Commercially prepared artist's casein is made from
kim milk that has been soured either naturally or by
he addition of a small amount of hydrochloric or other
cid. The whey is separated out, and the curd is thor-
ughly washed and dried. The product, a granular power, is casein.

Casein paint is made by mixing pigments with
asein powder in solution. The artist may use commer-
ally prepared casein paint that comes in tubes, or pre-
are his own paint in the studio. Since commercial
asein paint contains a high concentration of preserva-
ves as well as glycerine to retard hardening, many
rtists prefer to make their own. Whichever you choose,

4.
Casein

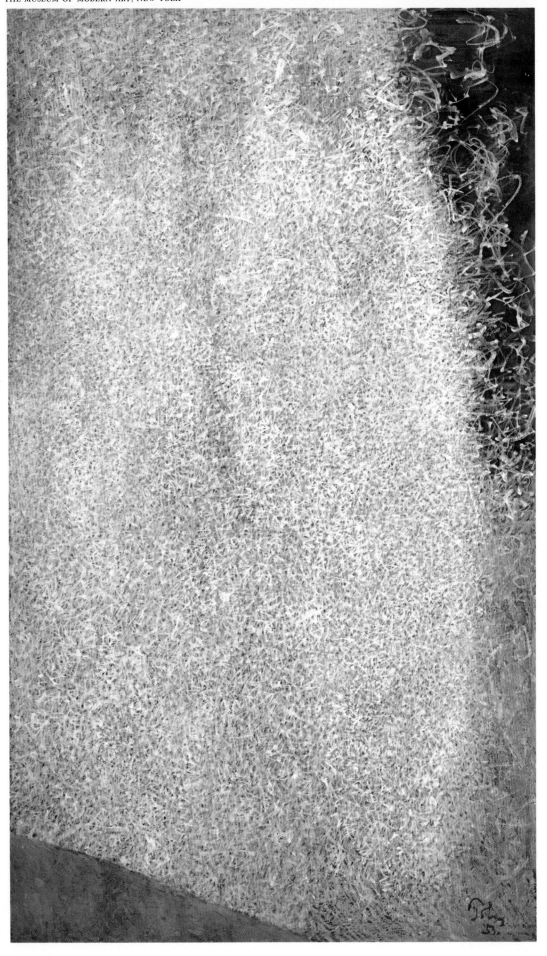

Edge of August by the twent
eth-century artist Mark Tobe
Casein on composition board.

At Five in the Afternoon, casein on cardboard, was painted by the contemporary artist, Robert Motherwell.

t is essential to remember that the technical dependability and permanence of the paint depend on its freshness. Dry casein must be stored in an airtight container and can be kept for only a few months — six at most; after that it is of little use to the artist. So, if you do not make your paint yourself, it is best to buy small amounts (enough to last three or four months) from a supplier who will guarantee its freshness at the outset.

THE CASEIN SOLUTION

To make casein solution, mix 4 ounces of casein powder with 22 fluid ounces (1⅜ pint) of water. Use a glass or enamel container and a wooden spoon. Leave the mixture to stand for an hour or so. When the casein has thoroughly soaked in the water, stir clear ammonia water drop by drop into the mixture until the casein has completely dissolved. The solution should have a thick, smooth, syrupy consistency, and it will give off an ammonia odor. If the solution is to be used in a gesso mixture, the ammonia will do no harm, but if it is to be used with pigments (or in emulsions for tempera), the ammonia should be driven off by evaporation. To do this, heat the solution in the top of a double boiler. Stir it continually until you can no longer smell ammonia. Do not allow it to boil.

69

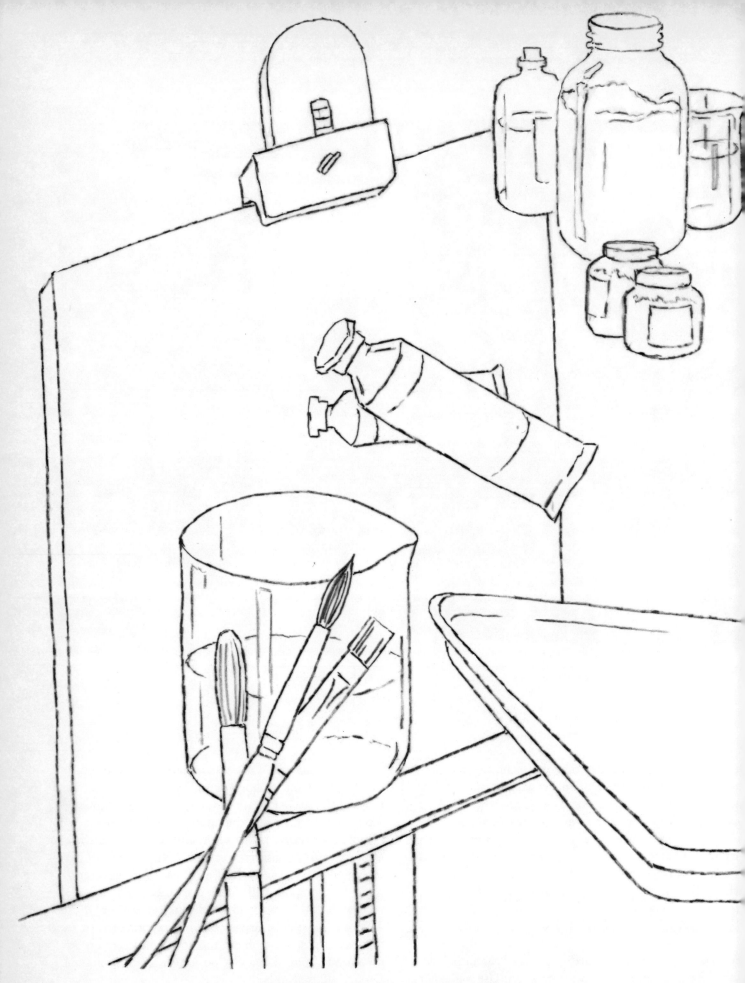

The basic equipment for preparing and painting with casein.

Casein solution cannot be stored for more than a few days unless a preservative is added. Sodium orthophenyl phenate, which is sold under the trade name Dowicide A, is most frequently used. Crush about ¼ teaspoon of this light powder in a few drops of water and stir it into the solution after it has cooled. The solution may then be stored undiluted in a covered jar.

PALETTE

The casein pigments are the same as those enumerated for watercolor (page 56), except when a lime casein is used. In this case, the list is limited to the fresco palette (page 78).

PREPARATION OF CASEIN PAINT

When the casein solution is to act as the binder for pigments, it may be used full strength or diluted to about two-thirds strength. To dilute the solution, add one part water to two parts casein solution — a maximum of 10 fluid ounces of water for a solution consisting of 4 ounces casein and 22 fluid ounces of water. Thus, the strength of the solution to be mixed with the pigments may range from 4 ounces of casein and 22 fluid ounces of water to 4 ounces of casein and 32 fluid ounces of water; the proportions depend upon your purpose and preference. Full strength, the paint will be thick and opaque — almost like oils; diluted, it will be thin and nearly transparent. Within this range, there is enough casein to bind the pigment, but not too much. To test for proper binding strength, mix the solution with a pigment and make a few brushstrokes. They should dry to a tough, hard film. If there is too much binder, the paint will crack and easily chip; if there is too little, the pigments will be powdery and rub off.

If you are going to paint on plaster walls, you can prepare the paint as just described or you can prepare a lime casein. Lime casein is made by grinding together five parts dry casein powder and one part slaked lime and diluting the mixture with four or five parts water. Mixed with fresco pigments and further diluted, it may be used on old plaster, moist fresco ground, or wet limewash.

SUPPORTS

Casein paint is relatively inflexible when dry, so it requires a rigid support. It works best on heavy illustration board, wallboard or walls, or gesso panels.

To make a gesso paste, mix undiluted casein solution with about 4 pounds of precipitated chalk. Then add about 1 quart (32 ounces) more water to thin the paste so that the gesso can be brushed on the support.

BRUSHES AND OTHER EQUIPMENT

Either sable or bristle brushes can be used with casein. Bristle brushes are best for heavier, impasto areas; large sables are preferable if the casein is thinned to a glaze, and small sable rounds are used for lines and fine details. The brushes should be carefully washed after each use.

A container of water is needed for thinning the paints and rinsing the brushes during the course of work. A slab of glass or china plate will serve as well as a manufactured porcelain or enamel palette. The palette, like the brushes, should be well cleaned after each use, since once casein paint has dried it is virtually insoluble and quite difficult to remove.

AN APPROACH TO PAINTING WITH CASEIN

Casein is a versatile medium that can be handled in a number of ways. It can be thinned with water and used as a wash like watercolor; casein washes are heavier bodied and lack the delicacy of watercolor, but since they become insoluble when dry, other washes or glazes can be freely brushed over them. Casein may also be applied in a slight impasto to create heavier, more opaque passages. When dry, these areas may be modified with a more transparent wash.

Casein is a broad, direct medium, most effective for paintings conceived in terms of bold, flat areas of heightened color. It does not lend itself well to elaborate brushwork or finicky detail. Used properly, casein produces strong, rich, luminous paintings.

Casein dries to a matte finish, and most artists prefer to leave the surface as is. However, when it has dried completely, the painting may be varnished. There are two reasons for doing this. First, the varnish protects the paint surface, especially important if it is not to be covered with glass. Also, a painting may, in some instances, call for the enamel-like finish and sheen of a varnish glaze rather than the natural matte surface.

The best varnish for glazing casein paintings is a mixture of dammar varnish and stand oil. Use about equal parts (fluid measure) of dammar varnish and stand oil to five or six parts of turpentine. Brush on a thin, even coat of the glaze with parallel brushstrokes. When the varnish has dried (which takes about twelve to twenty-four hours depending upon the proportions of the varnish ingredients, how thinly the varnish was applied, and the temperature and humidity), a second coat may be applied.

The simplicity, grandeur, and moving humanity of the frescoes of Masaccio (1401-1428) astonished his contemporaries and virtually revolutionized painting. This detail of a mother and child is from *St. Peter Distributing Alms*, painted in *buon fresco*.

INTRODUCING FRESCO

Fresco is inextricably bound to architecture: its sole use throughout its long history has been to decorate walls and ceilings. Without doubt, the best-known fresco in the world is Michelangelo's vast painting on the ceiling of the Sistine Chapel. Remarkable in its conception and unparalleled in its sheer technical virtuosity, this is one of the most awesome and magnificent works of human genius. Almost as well-known are Raphael's frescoes (also in the Vatican), particularly his *School of Athens.* Less known but deeply moving are Giotto's frescoes in the Arena Chapel in Padua, Masaccio's *Tribute Money,* and Piero della Francesca's *Resurrection.* All of these and countless other Renaissance frescoes are profound statements about the dignity of the human spirit. For this reason we tend to associate fresco with monumental art and highly serious subjects. Yet its early use was modest and domestic — akin to the present-day use of wallpaper.

Three thousand years before Michelangelo labored atop scaffolding in the Sistine Chapel at the command of Pope Julius II, the walls of an open, sun-filled, rambling palace at Knossos on the island of Crete were covered with frescoes. The king who commissioned these paintings may have been Minos, greatest of the powerful sea kings of the Aegean, who lived about 1500 B.C. and whose name has been given to the extraordinary Minoan culture. To the ancient Greeks, King Minos was already a legend, and a legend he remained until 1900, when Sir Arthur Evans dug into a hillside on Crete and uncovered the palace. With that, legend became history. The Minoans, it was learned, were unlike any other peoples of the ancient world. Secure on their island, enjoying prosperity and power based on energetic seafaring and surrounded by stunning natural beauty, they seem thoroughly to have delighted in life. If their art is to be believed, they enjoyed elegant fashions, athletic entertainments, and the beauties of nature. And apparently they invented fresco, primarily to beau-

5.

Fresco

Michelangelo (1475-1564) learned the fresco technique at the age of thirteen, when he was an assistant in the workshop of Ghirlandaio. Twenty years later he executed the magnificent frescoes on the Sistine Chapel ceiling. The detail above shows *The Temptation and Fall of Man.*

The fresco technique, apparently invented by the Minoans, was known to the Etruscans a millennium later, doubtless to the Greeks (although no Greek frescoes have survived), and to the Romans. At right is an Etruscan fresco of a flute player from the *Tomb of the Leopards;* it dates from the early fourth century B.C. Such paintings were sometimes executed directly on the stone walls of the tomb chamber. At far right is a Roman fresco of a maiden picking flowers, sometimes called *Flora.* From Pompeii, it was painted in the first century B.C.

tify the walls of their homes with scenes of processions, ritual-games, flowers, birds, and animals.

The domestic use of painting had requirements that were, to say the least, exceedingly difficult to meet, and no doubt it took artists many years to evolve an appropriate technique. First, the paintings had to be as permanent as the walls on which they were painted. Since they decorated homes, they had to withstand daily wear and tear as well as atmospheric changes. Fresco, which actually *becomes* part of the wall, was the answer. The other fundamental requirement of the paintings was that they have a uniformly dull, or matte, surface. They cover a large area and are viewed from many angles; on a glossy surface, light would create disturbing reflections and patches of glare. Fresco admirably satisfies this requirement, too, and the technique evolved by the ancient Minoans was subsequently used by the Greeks,

the Etruscans, and the Romans, passing on in time to the artists of medieval Italy, the Italian Renaissance, and the present.

In fresco, pigments are applied to a freshly plastered wall. The particles of color penetrate as the plaster dries and are locked between the plaster particles. There are two procedures for accomplishing this and hence two types of fresco paintings: these are *buon fresco* and *fresco secco.*

In *buon fresco,* pigments dissolved in water (with nothing else added) are applied to the plaster while it is still wet. Only the area that can be frescoed in a session is plastered, and at each session a new working area is plastered and painted. If a larger area has been plastered than can be frescoed, the excess plaster is removed and the wall plastered afresh at the next session. The joining lines between each plastered and painted area

Piero della Francesca's majestic *Resurrection*, painted about 1463. Like his other frescoes, it was broadly executed in *buon fresco* with finishing touches, parts of which have flaked off, in *fresco secco*.

Because of their monumental breadth and expressive nuances, Masaccio's Santa Maria del Carmine frescoes became a "source book" studied and copied by countless Renaissance artists, including Michelangelo. Illustrated is *The Tribute Money*.

This Roman fresco is an example of an "idyllic landscape." It is not an actual scene, but an arrangement of the elements of landscape — trees, hills, villas, temples — a refreshing wall decoration for the homes of wealthy city-dwellers.

are visible in the finished fresco and indicate not only which method was used but also how many sessions were needed to complete the work.

Most fresco is not *buon fresco.* A demanding technique, it was rarely attempted, and is confined to a few works by such early Renaissance masters as Giotto and Masaccio. Before their time, fresco involved painting some sections on the wet plaster and finishing the work and adding details after the plaster had dried. Increasingly, during the fifteenth century, fresco work was done wholly on dry plaster, and the pigments were mixed with size, curd, or egg, thus creating a watercolor, casein, or tempera film on the plaster.

In *fresco secco,* the entire wall surface is plastered and allowed to dry. Then, before painting begins, the area of wall to be painted is thoroughly dampened with water that usually contains slaked lime. The pigments are mixed with either limewater or a casein solution.

Although it is much the simpler method, *fresco secco* has several disadvantages. The paint is generally thinner than in *buon fresco,* so the result is somewhat less

full-bodied, and the lime or casein in the water may diminish the brilliance of the pigments. Finally, it is the less permanent of the two fresco techniques. In *buon fresco,* the pigments sink deep into the plaster and form a firm bond; in *fresco secco* they are bound only to the surface of the plaster and may flake off. This is dramatically demonstrated by a number of Renaissance paintings in which the two methods were combined. In Piero della Francesca's *Resurrection* in Borgo San Sepolcro, parts of which were painted on after the fresco was completed, for example, the spear held by one of the soldiers (the second from the right) is intact below, but the upper part of the shaft and spear head have flaked off, leaving only a shadowy impression of the form. Such deterioration is most frequently due to dampness, which is the result of faulty construction of the wall itself.

If the wall is sound, both kinds of fresco are quite dependably permanent. Pompeiian paintings, such as the *Idyllic Landscape,* were executed by applying a mixture of pigment and slaked lime onto a highly polished

77

ground of wet lime and marble dust. The picture was then painted over the background color with other pigments, which were also in a slaked lime vehicle. The Pompeiian frescoes are brilliant and in remarkably good condition. Admittedly, they were sealed up and protected by the eruption of Vesuvius in 79 A.D. The major frescoes have been removed to a museum, but many minor ones may be seen as excavation uncovered them. Many of these are exposed to the elements because the roofs of the buildings were destroyed by the eruption, but they are holding up well. One need only to examine the structural walls to see why. The Romans were superb masons.

PALETTE

The pigments that can be used in fresco painting are those that will not be affected by the alkaline action of lime. The list is further restricted to pigments that will not fade or darken in sunlight or darken in air that carries even a modicum of acid pollutants.

The earliest fresco palette was extremely limited. The Minoans used a red made from native earth containing iron oxide, a blue (called Egyptian blue) made from copper silicates, and ocher. Slate was used for black, lime for white. The Romans used lampblack and bone black instead of slate, and added native earth browns (umber and sienna), green earth *(terre verte)*, and azurite blue (a copper carbonate) to the palette. By the Renaissance, vermilion had been added to the reds in *secco* work, and Verona brown (which is burnt green earth) was added to the native earth browns. Lime white was replaced by *bianco sangiovanni* (which is calcium carbonate — a lime derivative), and a blue called smalt was made from cobalt.

The fresco palette today includes the iron oxides (Mars red, violet, yellow, and black, Indian red, Venetian red, English red), the umbers and siennas, ocher, cobalt blue and cerulean blue, green earth, viridian, and chromium-oxide green and cobalt green. *Blanc fixe* (artificial barium sulfate) and titanium white have also been added to the traditional lime white and *bianco sangiovanni*. To simplify matters, at least at first, limit your palette: a good assortment might include any one of the Mars reds, Mars yellow, violet, and black, cobalt blue, chromium-oxide green, and titanium white.

PREPARATION OF THE PIGMENTS

The pigments for fresco are ground with a little distilled water or limewater to a pastelike consistency and stored in jars. The paste should be covered with just enough water to keep it from drying out.

Ordinarily, instead of mixing colors on the palette, as is done in oil painting, the colors needed are mixed beforehand and the paste stored. Colors that are needed to cover a large area or that will recur throughout the fresco should be prepared in sufficient quantity — it is virtually impossible to match a mixed color exactly.

SUPPORTS

Frescoes traditionally are executed on walls, of course, but you may also fresco a smaller, portable surface constructed and finished to simulate a wall. Although far more cumbersome than a canvas or panel, the portable support can be constructed in the studio and transported elsewhere when the fresco is finished. Using a portable support, moreover, makes an excellent introduction to fresco. The ideal way to learn the basic techniques is to work with and observe a fresco painter: in no other medium is apprenticeship of such value — and in no other medium is it so difficult to come by. Therefore, the best alternative is described. When you have practiced preparing the support, plastering, transferring working cartoons, and last but not least, painting in fresco, a wall will be far less intimidating than it may seem at first.

The support must be large enough to provide a generous surface for the various fresco procedures, yet small enough that it can be made absolutely rigid without being excessively unwieldy. A good working surface is 9 or 10 feet square; the dimensions of the frame might

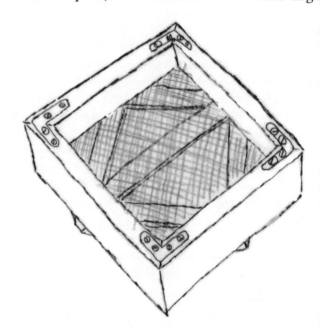

Fresco painting may be done on a portable support that consists of a frame with galvanized metal lath nailed to the underside. The frame is braced with crosspieces (as shown) or backed with a plywood panel; the lath is sandwiched between frame and braces or panel.

be 3 by 3 feet or 2½ by 4 feet. It is constructed of lumber that measures 1¼ by 2 inches or 2 by 4 inches, the 2-inch dimension being the depth of the frame in both instances. Galvanized metal lath is then nailed to the back. The frame is braced with crosspieces nailed or screwed to the frame, and angle irons can be used at the corners, if necessary. The lath is thus sandwiched between frame and braces. The frame must be absolutely stable. If it is not, the bracing is either faulty or inadequate and should be improved. Some artists prefer to back the frame and lath with a solid panel — ¾-inch plywood may be used. If this solid backing is employed, 1¼-by-2-inch lumber will be adequate for the frame. (Frames larger than those described and not backed by a solid panel should be made rigid by means of cradle bracework.)

The next step is to plaster the support. The plaster is mixed and applied in four successive layers.

The plaster for fresco is made of aged slaked lime and an inert aggregate such as sand or marble dust. You will need a wooden trough and a long-handled hoe for this. Slaked lime can be purchased in most building-supply stores, and few artists prepare their own. If it is not available, however, you can prepare it by mixing water (preferably distilled) with high-quality lime (calcium oxide). The water (approximately 1 gallon for each 10 pounds of lime) is added to the lime and mixed quickly. Be very careful not to spatter the lime as you add the water and mix, and work well away from any combustibles; the chemical reaction between the water and the lime generates intense heat. The consistency of the mixture should be liquid but not too thin. Vitruvius, the first-century Roman who wrote a treatise on building and related subjects, said that properly slaked lime should hang from the hoe like glue and be uniformly creamy, not lumpy.

The slaked lime is transferred to a storage box. Water is poured over it, the lid is fitted onto the box, and the box is buried in a pit below frost level. The slaked lime is then seasoned for at least six months — the longer, the better. A far better material is obtained if the aging is counted in years. The plasterers of ancient Rome required that it be aged at least three years, and it may have been the practice then, as it was later, to put down a large batch to age for use by the following generation. Modern fresco artists have affirmed that slaked lime that has been aged twenty-five years or more is far superior to "new" slaked lime. You can see why most artists nowadays leave the business of preparing slaked lime to the manufacturers of building supplies. But further seasoning of the purchased product is, of course, beneficial.

Slaked lime shrinks in drying and therefore will crack, so it is not ordinarily used alone as a plaster but mixed with inert aggregates to produce a stable material. As the plaster dries, the aggregate particles are bound together. Shrinkage cannot go beyond the point at which the particles are bound, although subsequent drying will bind them more firmly. The size of the particles is graduated from coarse to fine: the largest are about 1/16 inch in diameter, the smallest are roughly half this size. The aggregate must be absolutely clean, and free from salts, mica, clay, humus, or any other impurities. It must be absolutely dry when it is mixed with the slaked lime.

If the slaked lime has been stored long enough for a crust to have formed on the top, it should be strained before you mix it with the aggregates. The proportion of plaster to aggregate varies, depending on which layer of plaster is being applied; the amounts will be given below in the section on plastering the wall. The aggregates are turned and chopped into the plaster, and then the two are mixed thoroughly. No water is added in the mixing process, since it would dampen the aggregate particles and insulate them against the lime. You should make only as much plaster as you need for a specific plastering operation and use it immediately, but it will last a day or two if the trough is left covered.

If you are going to apply the plaster directly onto the face of a brick, stone, or hollow tile wall, thoroughly clean and inspect the surface. Hosing down and scrubbing it with a wire brush will remove dirt, old bits of plaster, and loose pieces of mortar. Any bricks that have traces of white efflorescence — "bloom," or "whiskers" — must be replaced. The whole surface must be uniformly porous or rough so that the plaster will adhere to it. If the surface is neither rough nor porous, you must hack it with a pick hammer to give it tooth, or texture. Before the first coat of plaster is applied, wet down the wall several times. The water soaks in with each dampening, until the wall has absorbed all the water it can hold.

Rather than plastering a structural wall itself, however, it is frequently more satisfactory to construct an inner wall (called furring) of framing strips and galvanized metal lath. This false wall, separated an inch or so from the exterior wall, is protected from any moisture that might penetrate the masonry of the building. The space also insulates the furring against great fluctuations of temperature, thus reducing the degree of expansion and contraction and further protecting the fresco. The frame and metal-lath furring is the most frequently employed; however, the second wall may be built of bricks or other material.

When the support has been prepared and — unless

it is of the frame and metal-lath sort — thoroughly soaked, it is ready for plastering. Four applications are needed. The accompanying cross section shows the composition and relative thickness of the layers of plaster.

The first, roughcast coat, or *trullisatio,* is a mixture of three parts coarse sand to one part slaked lime. The plaster should be of such a consistency that it will stand in a mound on the level trowel and just tend to run off if the trowel is tipped. If the plaster is not wet enough, water may be added. (Remember, the water may be added only at this stage, i.e., *after* the plaster has been thoroughly mixed and is ready for use, never during the mixing process.)

Throw the plaster on the wall, trowel-full by trowel-full, from a distance of about 2 feet, working from the bottom of the wall upward. Throwing the plaster prevents air bubbles from forming. Throw it at a slight

angle rather than straight on, otherwise bits will spatter back in your face. Apply the *trullisatio* to a thickness of about ¾ inch and spread it with the trowel. The surface should be even, but not overly smoothed. When the roughcast plaster has set (that is, it is firm but will take the impression of a fingerprint), which may take about twenty or thirty minutes, soak it. Now the second layer — the equalizing coat, or *arriciato* — is applied.

Mix the plaster for the second layer in the same proportions: three parts aggregate to one part slaked lime. If you use the same coarse sand as for the first layer, you can make enough plaster for both at the outset. If you use a slightly finer sand in the *arriciato,* you can clean out the trough and mix the mortar while the roughcast layer is setting. The *arriciato* is laid on in the same way as the preceding layer (or sometimes in two thin layers) to the same thickness, and then smoothed with a float. When it has set, wet it down and apply the third layer — the rough plaster, or *arenato.*

For the *arenato* the plaster consists of two parts of a finer aggregate or sand to one part lime. Lay it on about ½ inch thick, and smooth it. When it has set, it is moistened to receive the last layer — the fine plaster, or *intonaco.* The actual painting is done on the *intonaco.*

In *buon fresco,* only the section of the painting that can be completed in a day is given the *intonaco* coat, so only a small amount of plaster is mixed. For *fresco secco,* you need enough to cover the entire surface. The plaster for the *intonaco* consists of equal parts of lime and fine sand (or another fine aggregate, such as marble dust). It is applied to a thickness of only about ⅛ inch and smoothed with a float as well as a wet plane, so the surface is very smooth.

The thickness of the various layers of plaster may vary considerably, so that the total thickness is much more or somewhat less than the 2 inches just described. In general, the lean layers (in which there is proportionally more of the aggregate) are thicker; the fat layers (with proportionally more lime) are applied more thinly. The *intonaco* layer is always kept quite thin — never much more than ⅛ inch.

If you stop between applications of plaster for any longer than the time required for the preceding layer to set, a crystalline crust will form. This is removed with a metal scratching comb. The plaster is then thoroughly soaked, and the next layer applied.

It is possible to re-fresco a wall (or a portable support) by removing the last two layers of plaster — the *intonaco* on which the fresco has been done, and the *arenato.* These are chipped away as evenly as possible, the *arriciato* is thoroughly soaked, and the new *arenato* and *intonaco* layers are applied.

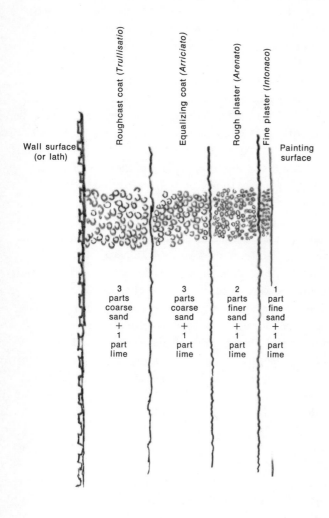

Cross section of a wall plastered for frescoing. The diagram shows the relative thickness of the layers of plaster, the relative size of the aggregates, and the composition of the plaster for each coat.

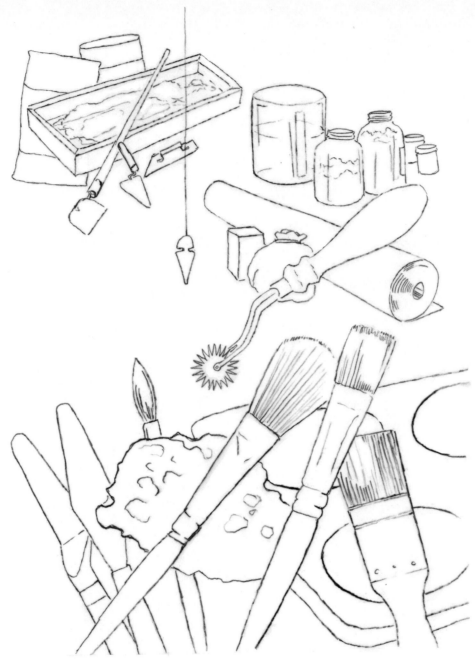

The basic equipment for fresco.

BRUSHES AND OTHER EQUIPMENT

Both bristle and hair (sable) brushes are used in fresco painting. Until the invention of the metal ferrule, the brushes used of course were rounds, and some fresco artists still prefer to use rounds exclusively. The sable brushes are reserved mainly for line work, cross-hatching, and the like. Bristles vary greatly in length, texture, and stiffness; the longer, softer bristles are best for fresco work.

Brushes that have been used with other media may be used for fresco painting, but they must first be thoroughly washed with soap and water, rinsed, and, for the best results, soaked in limewater for an hour or so before use. After each painting session, brushes must be carefully cleaned to remove all traces of lime; otherwise they will harden and be useless for further painting.

A sponge is also extremely useful for working the colors in fresco. It is dampened and used to blend color areas, soften the transitions between colors and contour lines, and generally unify the broad tones and values of the painting.

The best-known fresco in the United States is probably the vast fresco in the dome of the Capitol in Washington, D.C. Painted by Constantino Brumidi (1805-1880), it covers 4,664 square feet and is 180 feet above the rotunda floor The work is a prime example of illusionistic fresco. Brumidi, an Italian, was steeped in the style of the late Renaissance and baroque painters, who had created swirling visions of saints and angels in churches across Southern Europe. Translating the forms that had served religion into appropriate terms for a national monument, Brumidi depicted George Washington seated on a cloud surrounded by hovering figures personifying Liberty, Victory, and the thirteen original states. On a lower rank are six groups of figures representing War, Agriculture, Mechanics, Commerce, Naval Power, and the Sciences.

In addition, you will need a palette — an enamel one with depressions for the paint will serve. China plates are also quite satisfactory; some artists prefer them because they can be cleaned so easily. If you do *buon fresco*, you will also need a painting knife and a spatula for the joins in the plaster.

Of great value to the fresco artist is the plumb line — a device borrowed from the builder's art and used by the painter to establish true verticals wherever his composition requires them, for example, in representations of walls, buildings, and so on. Without doubt, the fresco artists of ancient Rome, who painted elaborate architectural motifs, used the plumb line, although no evidence exists to prove it except the frescoes themselves, and Renaissance artists certainly used this device. The Giotto frescoes in the Arena Chapel in Padua, for example, show marks indicating that plumb lines were snapped for true verticals, including the lines of buildings and the Cross. Apparently Masaccio was the first to use the plumb line to establish the vertical axis for standing figures. In his *Tribute Money* fresco (page 76), a vertical line that was established by a plumb line and scratched in the plaster runs through each standing figure from the head to the heel of the weight-bearing foot

AN APPROACH TO FRESCO PAINTING

Since a fresco painting is an integral part of a wall, it is most successful when it complements its architectural setting. It is always said that the design should enhance the flat wall surface rather than suggest the illusion of receding space, but this "rule," like any other that defines good design, has been broken time and again with impunity by individual artists and even by whole groups of artists. In fact, most of the frescoes we can still see are from periods in which illusionism reigned supreme The style of Roman fresco paintings, inherited from the Greeks, was highly illusionistic, capturing effects of light and shade, space and atmosphere. In the frescoes from Pompeii and Herculaneum, for example, columns, pilasters, and windows were painted in perspective to resemble actual architectural details, and within these "frames" the Romans painted illusionistic courtyards, buildings, or distant landscapes.

The next great period of fresco — perhaps the greatest — was the Renaissance, and the renewed pursuit of illusionistic realism may be traced from Giotto in the early fourteenth century through Giorgione, Leonardo, Raphael, and Michelangelo in the early sixteenth century. (The pursuit continued beyond the Renaissance of course, and reached its logical end in the photographic image in the nineteenth century.) Thus, the rule has been observed only by artists for whom il-

There has never been a great American tradition of fresco, but during the Depression of the 1930s there was a modest flowering under the government-sponsored Works Progress Administration. American artists decorated public buildings with murals, many of them executed in fresco. Illustrated is a detail of *Sweatshop* by George Biddle in the Justice Department Building, Washington, D.C.

Two frescoes and the squared preparatory drawings. Above, *The Monument to Sir John Hawkwood*, painted in 1436 by Paolo Uccello. This is the earliest complete extant preparatory drawing of its kind. Uccello worked out the design in a colored silverpoint drawing, which he then squared. By the end of the century, squared scale drawings were used commonly to facilitate enlargement. Below are *The Angel of the Annunciation* and the drawing, squared for transfer, by Pontormo (1494-?1557).

The Meeting of Joachim and Anna at the Golden Gate by Giotto (?1276-?1337). In the Scrovegni Chapel, Padua.

lusionism was irrelevant, as is the case today. *Trompe l'oeil* is out for the modern frescoist. That is, he must avoid the tricks of perspective, foreshortening, and modeling that create the illusion of three dimensions. Thus, today the effective fresco enhances the flat surface of the wall. It is designed in terms of broad, direct, and generally simplified forms that, though they may be representational, create an overall flat pattern. The interest and the impact depend upon the shapes and colors.

The work of the three modern masters of fresco —

the Mexican painters Diego Rivera, José Clemente Orozco, and David Alfaro Siqueiros — immediately reveals effective design better than words can. Their art is representational and intended to be an instrument of social reform. Rivera's frescoes treat revolutionary and political themes; Orozco's work is based on human sufferings, injustices and tyranny; Siqueiros, too, is profoundly concerned with the dilemmas of modern man as suggested by the title of his mural at the Polytechnical Institute in Mexico City, *Man the Master and not the Slave of the Machine.* (Interestingly, Rivera and

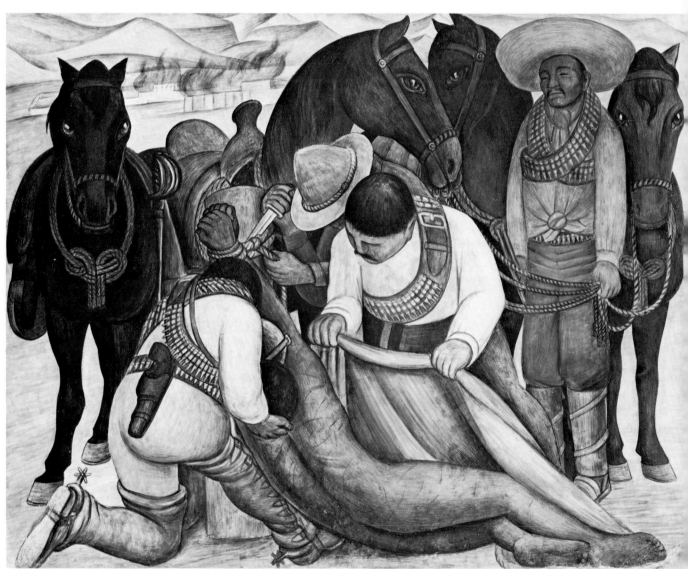

The greatest revival of fresco painting in this century was the work of Mexican artists, among them Diego Rivera (1886-1957) and José Clemente Orozco. Their murals, done in the United States as well as Mexico, were created as instruments of political and social reform. The subject of Rivera's *Liberation of the Peon*, painted in 1931, is the overthrow of the Díaz regime in Mexico and the rise of the peasant and worker class.

Dive Bomber and Tank by José Clemente Orozco (1883-1949) was painted in 1940. The fresco was executed on six panels, each 9 by 3 feet.

Orozco executed their works in the traditional fresco technique, whereas Siqueiros introduced into his work the distinctly modern synthetic paints.)

Working on so large a scale as a wall presents, in a medium that calls for rapid, decisive execution, means doing a great deal of careful preliminary planning. Although minor adjustments and changes can be made in the course of painting, the entire design — every detail and color area — is generally worked out ahead of time. Your initial ideas may be developed and refined in a series of rough pencil or pen sketches, as for any medium. When you have arrived at a satisfactory design, however, you then draw it to scale. If, for example, the area to be frescoed is 12 by 18 feet, the drawing might be 12 by 18 inches. Grid lines are ruled in on the completed drawing, dividing it into squares. The size of the squares will depend upon the scale you adopt. In the example given, a square inch on the drawing equals a square foot of wall surface, and the vertical and horizontal ruled lines should mark off 1-inch squares. The use of small scale drawings for fresco compositions dates back to about 1400. They were made not only as an aid for the artist but also to show to whoever commissioned the work. Only after the sketch was submitted and approved could the artist proceed with the work.

Some parts of the design will probably have to be worked out in greater detail than a small scale drawing

permits; these may be enlarged, perhaps to half the actual size. This is done by drawing a grid of 6-inch squares on another piece of paper and transferring the lines of the drawing marked off by the 1-inch squares to corresponding positions in the larger squares.

Generally, in addition to the detailed scale drawing, a full-color small scale version of the fresco is also done at the planning stage. The color sketch is usually done in watercolor, distemper, or gouache. All of the colors in the modern fresco palette are found also in the watercolor palette with the exception of the fresco whites, for which one of the watercolor whites must be substituted. If the fresco white to be used is *blanc fixe*, make a white that consists of one part titanium white to three parts *blanc fixe*. Since in gouache and distemper the pigments are mixed with varying amounts of white, these media most closely approximate the effects of the fresco colors. When they dry, fresco colors are lighter than when first applied, and this should be taken into account when you mix the colors for your sketch.

Now the design must be transferred onto the support. In Italy, where the great Renaissance frescoes were executed, paper was not introduced until about the beginning of the thirteenth century, and it remained a scarce commodity for at least a century. Thus, to arrive at the full-size working designs they needed, early Renaissance artists resorted to a method used by mosaicists. The entire design was sketched free-hand with a reddish

Andrea del Castagno (1423-1457) was commissioned to paint a fresco depicting *The Trinity and St. Jerome with Saints Paula and Eustochium* in the Church of Santissima Annunziata in Florence, and this painting provides a marvellous opportunity for the study of mid-fifteenth-century fresco techniques. One of the many frescoes damaged by the disastrous flood of 1966, it was removed from the wall to preserve it from further damage and for restoration. When the sinopia beneath it was revealed, it too was removed and remounted for better preservation.

The sinopia sketch was loosely done in charcoal on the *arenato*. The life-size figures of the three saints were drawn in completely; the Trinity was only schematically indicated. When the sinopia sketch had been completed, Castagno apparently was not satisfied, for he altered it significantly in the final painting. He gave much greater dynamism to the figures, particularly St. Jerome, by changing positions and gestures; these modifications were worked out in a full-scale cartoon, which was then transferred to the wall by pouncing. Although the cartoon has vanished, dotted marks outlining many of the shapes in the finished fresco are evidence of its use.

The painting was executed in *buon fresco* throughout. In the first "final" version, the entire figure of Christ was shown in extreme foreshortening. Once again the artist was dissatisfied — perhaps the foreshortening was awkward — so he painted seraphim in *secco* over the lower part of the figure. This addition, however, has largely peeled off, leaving only shadowy traces of the forms that once covered the loin cloth and legs of the figure of Christ.

brown pigment on the *arriciato* (or, if there was one, the *arenato*) layer of plaster. This sketch, called a sinopia drawing (from the ancient name of the pigment, which came from Sinope in Asia Minor), was covered over section by section by the *intonaco* layer of plaster. As each patch of plaster covered the lines beneath, the lines were redrawn on the new plaster.

Another method of transferring the design to the wall — the cartoon — came into use about the middle of the fourteenth century. The cartoon is a full-size drawing of the design to be transferred. To make a cartoon, cut strips from a wide roll of paper and rule them off in squares. Draw in the design section by section; be sure to put register marks along the edges of each section so that the strips can be aligned accurately. There are two ways to transfer the lines of the cartoon to the wall. You can trace over the lines with a pointed instrument, such as the handle end of a paint brush, so they are lightly incised in the soft plaster. The alternative is pouncing. Here you perforate the lines of the cartoon with a tracing wheel, fasten the cartoon against the wall, and force pounce (a very fine powder — frequently charcoal dust) through the perforations onto the wall. Tracing wheels, pounce, and pounce bags are manufactured commercially and are available through any art-supply store. Some artists use both incising and pouncing, the former to outline broad, simple shapes, the latter to define more detailed areas.

From the mid-fifteenth century onward, artists made use of whichever preparatory method suited them best. Benozzo Gozzoli, Paolo Uccello, and Andrea del Castagno worked out sinopia designs; Piero della Francesca and Domenico Ghirlandaio made extensive use of pounced cartoons. Andrea del Sarto, Melazzo del Forli, Pietro Perugino, Antonio Pollaiuolo, and Luca Signorelli frequently preferred to incise the design into the fresh plaster, sometimes free-hand, sometimes using a cartoon. Artists also combined or varied the methods as they saw fit. For example, in his frescoes in the refectory of the former convent of Sant' Apollonia in Florence, Andrea del Castagno used sinopia drawings on the rough plaster. However, he did not draw free-hand, as was traditional, but used pounced cartoons, which were again used on the final plaster.

In *fresco secco*, the entire surface to be frescoed is given the *intonaco* coat and allowed to dry. The plaster is then thoroughly saturated, and the colors, mixed in a lime-water (or limewater and casein) solution, are applied.

In *buon fresco*, of course, only that section of the design to be painted is given the *intonaco*. Apply the *intonaco* plaster beginning at the top of the area to be frescoed and, session by session, work downward. This prevents the sections already painted from being splattered by wet plaster or paint during subsequent sessions.

You cannot start to paint until the plaster becomes firm. When it no longer gives way under light pressure of a finger (about fifteen or twenty minutes), you can transfer the cartoon by tracing or pouncing, and begin painting. The pounced or incised lines may be painted in boldly — preferably with a color such as ocher or red oxide, which will not interfere with the colors subsequently applied.

Lay in large color areas at one time. They may be brushed on in a single application if the color has the desired intensity, or built up to the desired effect with several washes. The local colors are then broadly related and modified by sponging and contrasting washes, overpainting and the addition of other details, such as crosshatching. Lastly, dark and light accents — shadows and highlights — are added.

While you must concentrate on one area at a time, each must be handled in relation to those previously painted and those yet to be painted. In your mind, at least, you should "see" all the parts of the fresco developing simultaneously. You should constantly check whether or not the parts are relating satisfactorily to each other so that the completed painting will present a unified whole; step back frequently and view the overall effect, visualizing the areas as yet unpainted.

You must stop painting when carbonation of the setting plaster begins to form a lime crust on the surface. At this point, the brush will drag and the colors soak into the surface too quickly, becoming hard to work. Cut away any unpainted *intonaco* plaster with a palette knife. Undercut — or bevel — the painted section all along the edge where the next application of plaster will begin. When you are ready to proceed, wet the edge thoroughly, apply the plaster (the new plaster will fill in the undercutting along the border), and smooth the surface seam with a spatula so it is as invisible as possible. The seam should follow a line in the drawing or the edge of a color area rather than cut across an area of solid color — since the join cannot be completely obscured, it should at least be unobtrusive.

Areas that have been painted but are not satisfactory cannot be reworked after the lime crust begins to form and should also be cut away. However, minor corrections and retouching may be done after the fresco has dried completely (this will take at least a month). Casein, distemper, or egg tempera may be used; casein is best because the colors and matte effect of the medium are closest to fresco. However, retouching should be kept to a minimum, since neither in color nor permanence do any of the media approach the quality of fresco.

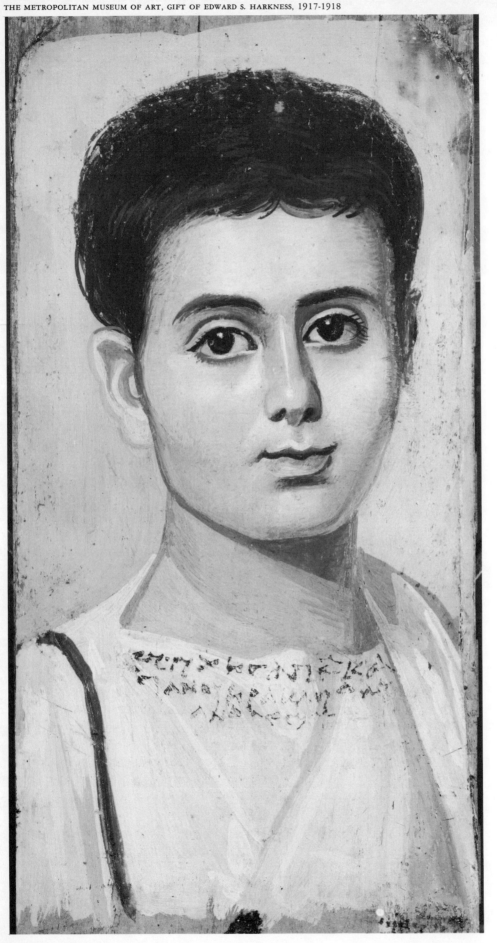

Greek and Roman encaustic paintings have perished; we know of them only by report. The oldest extant examples of encaustic are a group of paintings done in Egypt early in the Christian era. Called the Fayum portraits, these likenesses of persons who had died were attached to their mummies and entombed with them.

INTRODUCING ENCAUSTIC

The term "encaustic" comes from the Greek *enkaustikos,* "to burn in." In his *Natural History*, written about 70 A.D., Pliny described encaustic as "To paint with wax [colors], and to burn in the picture." Pliny mentioned three different processes. In one, the pigments mixed in wax were spread on the support and smoothed with a *cestrum,* a spatula-like implement. In a second, a wood or ivory surface was covered with a wax color, and the design was incised with a stylus. Then, the incised lines were probably filled in with colors, given a wax varnish, and heated. The third technique described by Pliny is encaustic as we generally use it today: it involved mixing pigments with wax that is in some manner dissolved or liquefied, applying the colors on the support with a brush, and burning in, or heating the finished surface to fix or fuse the colors.

Encaustic painting was practiced by the ancient Greeks. Evidently, the manner of encaustic painting that employed liquefied wax applied with a brush was first used in ship-painting — not as decoration but, in Pliny's words, as "proof against the sun's heat, the salt of the sea, and the winds." The wax, mixed with resin, was used as a varnish to waterproof and protect the wooden planking. From this the encaustic medium may have evolved, for from the purely practical technique of painting with wax it was but a short step to the decorative. The wax and resin varnish was used as a vehicle for colors, and decorations were painted on the ships in conjunction with the preservative varnishing. Pliny mentions two Greek painters who began as ship decorators. And in time, wax painting was practiced in its own right, to produce small panel pictures. Two fourth-century Greek artists, Pausias and Nicias, were famous for their encaustic paintings and they are said to have achieved a highly realistic style through subtle gradation of tones, the use of light and shadow, foreshortening, and other artistic devices.

6.

Encaustic

Harlequin by the contemporary artist Karl Zerbe. Encaustic.

The Storm by contemporary artist Karl Zerbe was done in encaustic on backed canvas.

None of the Greek encaustic panels has survived except in the admiring accounts of Romans who wrote about the technique and also practiced it. None of the Roman encaustic panels has survived either, but many produced in Egypt under Roman occupation have. These are the so-called Fayum portraits. Dating between 100 and 250 A.D., they are the earliest extant painted portraits and the only extant examples of a technique widely practiced in the ancient world.

In Egypt the encaustic technique, like so much else, served the dead. The portraits were likenesses of persons who had died, and they were attached to the mummies, held in place by the bandaging around the head and shoulders. Encaustic continued to be practiced in the early centuries of the Christian era. It is mentioned in an eighth-century manuscript, but apparently by that time it was little used, and subsequent references to it are scattered and vague.

The ancient method of true encaustic painting was forgotten until about the middle of the nineteenth century, when some artists made concerted attempts to resurrect it. Classical and medieval accounts were carefully studied and compared to reconstruct the materials and techniques. The research has continued, and although encaustic is not widely practiced, a number of modern artists have used it successfully, the best-known being Karl Zerbe.

There are many reasons why painters have devoted

93

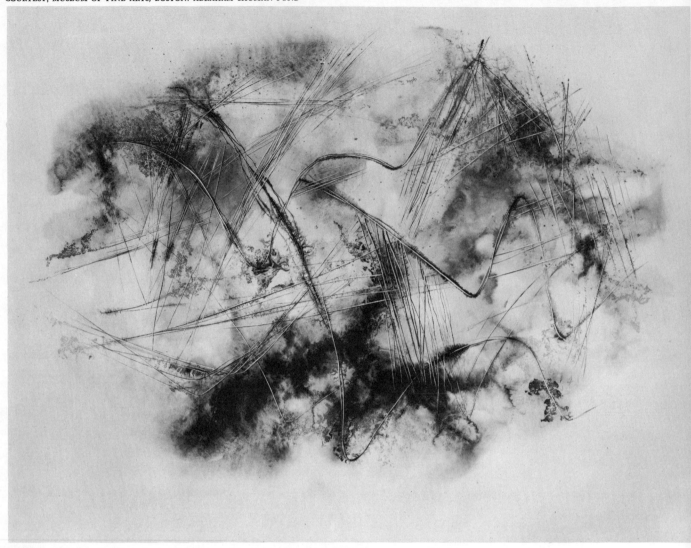

Mountain Landscape, an encaustic painting by Esther Geller, who studied the technique with Karl Zerbe.

themselves to uncovering the secrets of encaustic. Wax has enticing qualities to recommend it as a binder: one is permanence. It does not yellow or oxidize with age, and it is not affected by moisture. Encaustic colors have a remarkable brilliance, and the surface of the finished painting may be polished to produce an enamel-like sheen. A wide range of effects is possible — opaque and transparent color, glazes, and high impasto.

Encaustic will not appeal to every painter. The technique requires more equipment than any other. Although there are a number of highly satisfactory recipes for making the binder and ways to use the paint, none can claim with authority to be "authentic." Of course, with every medium there is a great deal of room for experimentation and discovery, but in no other are the original equipment, recipes, and procedures so complex and conjectural. For some artists, however, the pleasure of research into ancient accounts and study of the remarkable Fayum portraits make encaustic irresistible; so it is, too, for those who love a challenge and have the patience to pursue the magic results.

PALETTE

One advantage of encaustic is that a wide range of pigments may be used. The palette comprises the permanent pigments in both the watercolor and oil palettes (see pages 56 and 118), as well as a number of the unstable organic and inorganic pigments.

PREPARATION OF THE PIGMENTS

One way of preparing encaustic colors is to combine each dry, ground pigment with melted wax — pure, sun-bleached beeswax — and to pour the liquid color into a form or mold to cool and harden. The cakes or blocks of wax color may be used immediately or stored indefinitely.

The alternative ways of preparing the pigments involve combining the pigments with a binder. Wax is the primary substance in the binder, but it is generally mixed with a resinous substance or oil to give it durability. The wax, when dry, will protect the pigments, but adding a small amount of resin or oil modifies the undesirable qualities of wax — it hardens the surface permanently so it will not simply remelt when heated and will resist scratches and abrasions.

We do not know whether the artists of the classical period added resin or oil to the wax or used wax alone. It is logical to suppose that a hardening agent was added; however, some authorities have analyzed the Fayum portraits and have found no evidence to support this. How, then, was the permanence of the paintings achieved? It has been suggested that some sort of wax emulsion was involved, and a number of modern artists, including Karl Zerbe, have used wax emulsions in their encaustic work. But we really don't know how the classical Greek and Roman artists actually prepared their wax binder. Admirable results can be achieved in a number of ways — the wax and resin or oil mixture will be described here.

The wax must be pure, sun-bleached beeswax. You

In his startling *Target with Four Faces* — a mixed media work — the contemporary painter Jasper Johns used encaustic over collage on canvas. The faces are plaster casts.

95

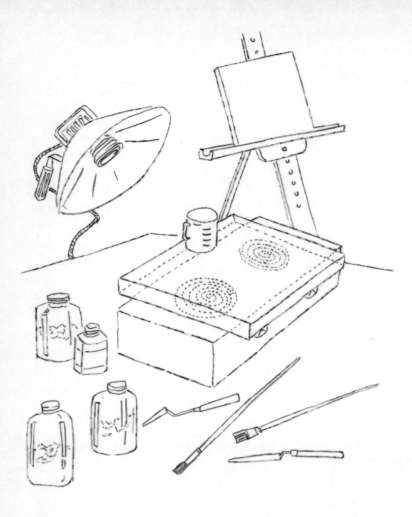

The basic equipment for work in encaustic.

can use dammar varnish (a resin), sun-refined linseed oil, or a combination of the two. If dammar varnish is used, it may be thinned slightly with turpentine to a more workable brushing consistency: add about one part turpentine to three or four parts dammar before combining the varnish with the wax. The proportions of the wax mixture are about four parts melted wax to one part either resin or oil. The amount of resin or oil or the two combined should not exceed a third of the mixture.

Heat the lump wax over a low flame or on an electric plate. A tin measuring cup is a good container — add wax until the level of the liquid wax reaches just over the three-quarter mark. Then add enough oil or resin (about 3 or 4 tablespoons) to raise the contents to a level cupful. The binder will harden when it is allowed to cool, but reheating will liquefy it again. It may be kept for a few days, but if you make only the amount needed for each working session, you will ensure the freshness of the oil.

If you have combined the pigments with wax to make blocks or sticks of color, when you are ready to work you simply melt as much as you need on the palette, add oil or resin to the pool of wax color, and mix it with a spatula. If you have prepared the binder separately, put the dry pigments on the palette, heat the binder until it has melted, and add it to the colors. With the spatula, mix them to a creamy consistency. If you will need a large amount of a particular color in a given session, you can mix it all at once and keep it warm in a small tin container on a corner of the palette.

SUPPORTS

The support for encaustic should be rigid rather than flexible. A wood panel is generally preferable, although Masonite may be used. Give the panel a gesso ground, as described on page 106. You can use canvas if you wish, but it should be backed with a rigid support. The canvas should be sized and primed with a thin ground as described on page 122.

BRUSHES AND OTHER EQUIPMENT

Bristle brushes are used in encaustic painting. An assortment of five or six of various sizes should be selected and used exclusively for encaustic work. Clean the brushes after each use by warming them to liquefy the binder imbedded in the bristles and wiping them with a clean, absorbent rag, pressing gently to blot up the paint. Then rinse them in turpentine, and wipe and blot again.

You will also need palette and painting knives for mixing the pigment and binder, applying the paint to the support, scraping paint off areas to be reworked, and scraping the palette clean after a working session.

The encaustic palette differs from those used with other media in that it must be of a material that can be heated uniformly, and it is used with a two-burner electric hot plate. The hot plate must have switches that dependably regulate the heat at low, medium, and high on both burners. The palette is made of metal and can easily be made to order by a metalworker. It must be constructed to sit over the burners, not directly on them. It is simply a shallow metal box that is inverted over the burners; the sides should be about 2 inches high to allow space for the heat to circulate evenly. The bottom of the box (which, when inverted over the burners, becomes the palette surface) should be of ¼-inch-thick steel. The four sides may be either steel or iron and of a smaller gauge. A complete encaustic palette and heating unit is also available commercially and may be ordered directly from the manufacturer or through an art supply store.

A heat lamp with heating coil mounted on a reflector bowl is the simplest device to use and the easiest to obtain for burning in the picture. Some artists prefer to use a blowtorch, but unless this tool is expertly handled it can cause fire or injury, and so it is not recommended.

AN APPROACH TO ENCAUSTIC PAINTING

The encaustic painting may be planned in a series of drawings, the final one being sketched onto the gesso ground. The heated (liquefied) colors are applied to the ground with brushes or painting knives. The paint may be applied thickly or thinned somewhat with turpentine. The colors will harden as soon as they are laid on, but reworking and blending are possible if the ground is warmed with the lamp. Since the paint does harden immediately, rapid application of direct color, overpainting in scumbles, and glazes in quick succession are all possible.

To make changes and corrections, you can remove paint areas by heating them and scraping the colors off with a palette knife. With practice, you will learn to use the heat lamp frequently to give flexibility to the application and responsiveness of the paint.

To burn in the colors, lay the painting flat and, holding the heat lamp about six inches above the surface, move it slowly back and forth. As it is heated, the paint will penetrate into the ground and fuse. It should not be heated so much that it bubbles or runs.

You can work on the painting further after it is burned in. When you have finished and burned in the color for the last time, the paint begins to age and set to a tough, durable surface.

Left to right, details from *The Storm* (page 93), *Mountain Landscape* (page 94), and *Target with Four Faces* (page 95).

  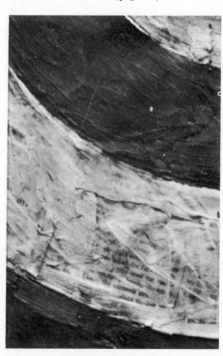

Detail from *Salome Dancing Before Herod*, a panel painted in tempera by an unknown Catalan artist in the mid-fifteenth century.

INTRODUCING TEMPERA

Perhaps the most satisfying introduction to tempera is to stand before such a work as Duccio's *Maestà*: here is a purity of color, an iridescence of tone that can scarcely be imagined and can never be described. Tempera was a common medium for four hundred years, from the twelfth through the fifteenth century, and the artists, like Duccio, who practiced it were consummate craftsmen.

Tempera reigned supreme in Europe until the advent of oils during the fifteenth century. Then, the two techniques were combined so freely that in many cases we cannot now tell how paintings of the time were painted. Of the fifteenth-century works reproduced on the following pages, Sassetta's *Journey of the Magi* is in tempera alone. Oil glazes and tempera were used alternatively, and details might be finished in either medium. In some works, tempera was used for the underpainting and the remainder of the painting was done entirely in oil, so that all traces of the tempera were obscured. Other works were done in tempera, with oil glazes added to unify the color and brushwork. This is the technique used by Veneziano in the small panel painting, *St. John in the Wilderness*. In still others, oil impasto was laid over the tempera to produce broad modeling effects; such touches were frequently added a later hand. (This is true of the oil overpainting done on Mantegna's *Triumph of Caesar*. This cycle of paintings was executed in tempera, but the additions in oil leave little of the original tempera visible.)

As oil painting waxed, tempera waned. Pure tempera painting was not practiced beyond the turn of the sixteenth century, although tempera continued to be used as an adjunct to oil painting (for sketches and underpainting) into the seventeenth century. El Greco, for instance, used tempera in this fashion. But by 1700

7.

Tempera

The small tempera panel of *The Journey of the Magi* (above) by the Sienese painter Sassetta (1392-1450) is imbued with the charm and delicacy of a late Gothic illumination.

This little panel of *St. John in the Desert*, part of a large altarpiece, was painted by Domenic Veneziano, who worked in the mid-fifteenth century. Veneziano experimented with oils which he used in glazes over tempera.

tempera was passé, and so it remained for almost 150 years — until, in the midst of a passion for the past and a rapid succession of "revival" styles, the writings of Cennino Cennini were first translated into English and the techniques of tempera were rediscovered.

Tempera is a demanding medium, not well suited to the needs of hasty expression or dilettantism. But the effects it is capable of producing have won it ardent admiration, and from time to time artists have returned to it, preferring it to all other media. In our time it has been revived, most notably in the work of Ben Shahn, who said: "I like painting that is tight and clear and under control. That's why I use tempera instead of oil. It's too easy to paint out your mistakes in oil."

Tempera lends itself best to precise areas or patterns of colors. Its overall tonality is cool; it cannot successfully convey the expressive warmth of oils. Transitions from value to value and color to color must be planned

In the seventeenth century, Andrea Mantegna (1431-1506) produced a tour-de-force cycle of tempera paintings — an 80-foot-long procession of nine 9-foot-square canvases called "The Triumph of Caesar." Illustrated is *The Picture Bearers.*

This poignant *Cherubs and Children* was painted by Ben Shahn (1898-1969).

and precise, while in oils such transitions may be virtually imperceptible. But the luminous freshness, clarity, and sparkle of tempera colors are incomparable, and in tempera, shapes may be rendered broadly or elaborated in infinitely painstaking detail. The medium might be likened to *bel canto* singing with its disciplined precision apparent in every note (oils, though capable of precision to some degree, are more like operatic drama, ballads, or rock-and-roll). Tempera does not lend itself to naturalism. It is suited, rather, to formality and abstraction, in which the artist selects from, reduces, reformulates, or transforms the surface appearance of things in terms of interrelated forms. It is a cerebral medium. This does not mean that the artist working in tempera must be an intellectual, but that he aims at clarity rather than ambiguity, contained expression rather than dramatic pathos, idea and essence rather than subjective experience.

The term "tempera" is decidedly confusing. We take it to refer to a specific medium, but historically it has been used to refer to any agent that binds pigments. Thus, mixing pigments with any binder, whether size, gum, glair (egg white), egg yolk, or even oil, is "tempering." When Cennino Cennini used the word "tempera," sometimes he meant only "binder," but when he used it to describe some kind of emulsion, he meant what we now understand to be true tempera.

The special basis of tempera is the emulsion. Broadly speaking, an emulsion consists of globules of one kind of liquid evenly suspended in another. For example, milk is a natural emulsion in which tiny particles of butterfat are suspended in an aqueous solution. The yolk and the white of eggs are natural emulsions too: both consist of oil particles suspended in an aqueous solution of albumen. Artists have variously used the yolk, the white — and even the whole egg — as bind-

102

ers. In the yolk, however, the proportions of the various substances seem best suited to the artist's needs. The yolk is composed primarily of roughly 50 percent water, 15 percent albumen, 22 percent fat or oil, and 9 percent lecithin — a fatlike substance that actually absorbs and retains moisture and also behaves as an emulsifier.

As tempera dries, the water evaporates and the albumen hardens, forming a viscous film around the oil particles suspended in it. The result is a tough, hard surface film that is relatively insoluble in water. Glair (binder made of the white of the egg alone) is less tough and more readily soluble than egg-yolk binder because the white contains proportionately less oil than the yolk (84 percent water, 12 percent albumen, and .2 percent fat).

The most widely used emulsion in tempera is egg, but artificial emulsions may be formed from resins such as gum arabic, from wax, and from other substances.

PALETTE

Pigments that tend to be opaque rather than transparent are best suited to tempera painting. Since it is necessary to grind and handle the dry tempera pigments, those that are poisonous must be eliminated from the palette. This is unfortunate: white lead (flake white and Cremnitz white), from many points of view the most satisfactory white, is highly poisonous. But there is virtually no foolproof way to handle it. Sooner or later, ground particles may be inhaled and minute traces may get under fingernails. Once lead has entered the body, it remains there — and accumulates. For this reason, never use white lead and lead compounds, or the arsensic compounds, in tempera — or any other work in which dry pigments are handled. The following must therefore be eliminated from the tempera palette: Naples yellow (lead antimoniate), chrome yellow (lead chromate), chrome green (a mixture of the poisonous lead-chromate yellow with a blue pigment), emerald green (copper aceto-arsenite), and cobalt violet (cobalt arsenite).

Except for the pigments that must be eliminated because of their toxicity, the tempera palette may include all the colors listed for oils (page 118). However, the best pigments for tempera are the most opaque: the cadmium reds and red oxides (including the Mars, English, and Indian reds); ocher, the cadmium yellows and Mars yellow; cobalt blue and cerulean blue; chromium-oxide green; and Mars violet.

Blacks and whites are very important in tempera painting. They are mixed with the other colors to obtain dark and light values. The blacks — ivory black, Mars black, lampblack — have a clearer, richer quality in tempera than in oil painting; mixed with white, they produce grays that are pure and distinctive. Ivory black is a good all-purpose black, and either titanium white or zinc white may be selected. Titanium white is slightly more opaque than zinc white.

PREPARING THE EMULSION

The pigments may be ground into a paste with water alone, with egg-yolk emulsion, or with a mixture of the emulsion and water. If there is any yolk in it, the paste will be usable only so long as the yolk is good, so less paste is prepared. If the pigments are ground in water alone, the paste will keep indefinitely (if you pour a little water over it to keep it from drying out).

The emulsion is prepared as follows: Separate the yolk of the egg from the white. Holding the yolk over a jar, puncture the yolk sac, let the yolk run out, and discard the sac. A small amount of water (about ¼ teaspoon) may be stirred into the yolk. Emulsion left over after a painting session will keep for three or four days under refrigeration. Preservatives such as vinegar, realgar (red sulfide of arsenic), acetic acid, phenol, or oil of cloves have sometimes been added to retard spoilage; however, it is preferable to prepare a small amount of emulsion and use it while it is fresh. If the emulsion does spoil, it is of course discarded, as is the jar in which it was stored. A new mixture will spoil more quickly if put in that same container.

When you are ready to begin painting, put a small amount of pigment paste on the palette, add emulsion, and combine them with a palette knife. There should be roughly equal amounts of paste and emulsion. It is important to use the right amount of emulsion; some pigments will require more than others. When pigment and emulsion have been mixed, test the paint by brushing a few strokes on a nonporous surface such as a glass slab or china plate. The paint should dry to a tough film with a slight sheen, and you should be able to peel it off in a single piece by lifting an edge with a knife or razor blade and pulling up. If the film breaks apart or flakes, or if the paint is dull or chalky, there is not enough egg to bind the pigment adequately and you should add more emulsion. If the paint will not brush out smoothly and dries immediately, there is too much emulsion and you should add more pigment.

The egg-yolk emulsion has been described because it is the most common as well as the "classic" form of tempera. As noted at the beginning of this chapter, however, the basis of tempera is the emulsion, and many kinds of emulsion are possible. An egg-and-oil emulsion consists of egg combined with stand, linseed, or sun-thickened oil, Venice turpentine or dammar varnish, and water. A gum-arabic emulsion is a solution of gum arabic and stand oil or stand oil and dammar varnish. Wax emulsion is made from saponified wax (wax soap) combined with egg, gum, glue, or varnish solution, and casein emulsion is made by combining casein powder with wax soap or with dammar varnish or Venice turpentine. For precise recipes, the reader is referred to the indispensable book by Ralph Meyer, *The Artist's Handbook* (see Bibliography).

SUPPORTS

A rigid support has always been considered the best for painting in tempera. Flexible supports such as paper and canvas have also been used, but generally for a specific reason. An interesting example is the *St. Mary Magdalen with a Crucifix* (page 28) by Spinello Aretino, which was made as a banner to be carried in processions. When dry, tempera film is not flexible, as oil paint is, and may crack. Therefore, if you prefer to work on a textile or paper surface, it should be mounted on a firm support.

Traditionally, the tempera support was a panel made of well-aged wood with a minimum of grain. In Italy, poplar was most frequently used, while in northern Europe, oak and later mahogany were preferred. Among other woods used were beech, cedar, chestnut, fir, larch, linden, olive, pine, and walnut. Several pieces were joined to make large panels, and frequently several plies were used to prevent cracking or warping. The panel was leveled with a plane and sanded. Gesso, a mixture of plaster of Paris and glue, was then applied either directly on the wood surface or on finely woven linen that had been stretched over the panel. After several thin coats of gesso had dried, the surface was smoothed with a fine abrasive. If there was to be a gold background, as was usually the case, the surface had to be further treated so the tissue-thin gold leaf would adhere. Over the gesso the artist applied a size, which consisted of one or more coats of "bole," a red clay thinned with water. Area by area the gold leaf was applied to the moistened surface of the bole-covered gesso panel. The gold leaf, too delicate to handle with the fingers, was picked up with a broad, soft-haired brush that had been drawn lightly over the face (this process charged the brush hairs with static electricity). When the size was dry, the overlapping edges of gold leaf were brushed off, and the gold surface was burnished to a beautifully rich sheen.

Many painters who use wood panels today prefer to look for old, and hence well-aged, wood — old table tops, for instance. Other wood must be thoroughly and properly seasoned. If you obtain it "dried" from a lumber company, be sure it has been dried by aging, not in a kiln. Even if the wood has been properly seasoned, it should be allowed to age further in the studio. After several months, when the planks seem stable, they may be made into panels. Plane the working surface smooth and set the panels aside for a few months more before use. If slight warping occurs, plane the wood smooth again and season it some more. Even very old wood may warp somewhat after the surface is planed down, so seasoning is essential.

There are a number of ways to minimize warpage, including laminating, bracing, or cradling. To carry out any of these successfully requires far more than knowledge of the technique. It calls for a craftsman's (not a carpenter's) understanding of woods and how to handle them. The best way to acquire this kind of understanding is to seek out a craftsman who will explain and demonstrate what is involved — the age-old apprenticeship method. There are no shortcuts.

Such a painstaking approach to making panels is attractive and practical only for a few. Most painters choose alternative supports, even though they are admittedly less satisfactory. One possibility is laminated panels — the universally available plywood. Much plywood is manufactured with badly or unevenly seasoned woods, little care to the proper running of the grain in the various layers, and inferior glues. As a result, the outer layers may buckle and several layers may even come apart completely. Thus, you should find out which plywoods are manufactured consistently and dependably well, and use them; they are more expensive, but the investment is well worth it.

The plywood should be from three- to five-ply, and ¼ inch to ¾ inch thick; the five-ply, ¾-inch type is best. The best facing, or outer ply, is birch. This is the working surface. It should be a single piece, not joined, and the grain should be as unobtrusive as possible. (Nearly all plywoods are available with either one side or both sides "good." The latter is more expensive, of course, and not necessary for painting panels.)

Masonite can be used for panels, but this is the only one of many types of wallboard manufactured for building purposes that is satisfactory. It is made from wood that has been reduced to pulp under steam pressure and then pressed into sheets with heat. Aside from a small amount of size added to make the board moisture-proof, it contains no special adhesives or other materials. The wood fibers apparently are bound together again by lignin, the substance that holds the cellulose cells together in all wood. Assuming that the quality of Masonite remains as high as it has been in the past, it may be recommended without qualification.

Masonite is available at almost any lumber company.

This panel depicting *The Birth of the Virgin* is from a mid-fourteenth-century altarpiece by Bernardo Daddi. Before the tempera painting was begun, gold leaf was applied to the gesso panel within the three scallops at the top of the ornamental frame and on the two halos, and the border was tooled with punches that impressed patterns on the surface.

The standard — and for the artist's purposes, most useful — thickness is ⅛ inch. It comes in 4-foot-wide sheets of various lengths.

Masonite is not only moisture-resistant; since it lacks the grain of natural wood, it also resists warping. It does not crack, and it expands and contracts only slightly. In short, it is a remarkably stable surface. Masonite panels should be handled carefully, however, because corners and edges chip rather easily. Also, large panels will bend and sag if stood on end, so if your painting is to measure more than about 2 feet along either dimension, the panel must be braced on the back. Glue on crossbars and strips of wood around the edges and clamp them until dry. The larger the panel, the more elaborate and heavier the bracing needed.

The two surfaces of Masonite are distinctly different — one is slick to the touch, the other rough. Most artists prefer to paint on the smooth side, although the reverse may also be used. The smooth side should, before painting, be rubbed well with a cloth saturated with a solvent, such as turpentine, or sanded — or both. This cleans the surface thoroughly of any traces of dirt and grease and gives it a tooth, which ensures a firm and even bond between the support and the gesso ground.

When the panel has been prepared, wipe it with a clean cloth to remove all traces of the dust from sanding and apply a coat of glue size. This is made by soaking 2½ or 2¾ ounces of powdered or granulated rabbit-skin glue in a quart of cold water for several hours (until all of the glue is thoroughly soaked) and then slowly heating the mixture just until the glue is dissolved. Do not allow it to boil. When it has cooled slightly, brush it on the panel.

There are a number of satisfactory recipes for gesso, including Cennini's mixture of parchment scraps, glue, and plaster of Paris, as well as combinations of other inert white pigments with such binders as gelatin and casein. A simple one is as follows: Prepare glue water by soaking 2¾ ounces of dry rabbit-skin or calfskin glue in a quart of cold water for several hours, until the glue is thoroughly saturated and swollen. Slowly heat the mixture in the top of a double boiler until the glue is dissolved. Do not permit it to boil. For a quart of the glue-and-water solution, you will need 3 to 4 pounds of filler. This may consist entirely of whiting, or nine parts whiting to one part either dry titanium or zinc-oxide white pigment. Combine the filler and the glue solution while the glue is still hot enough to be liquid. Some artists add the glue slowly to the filler, stirring steadily until the gesso has a smooth, creamlike consistency, and then strain it through cheesecloth to remove any remaining lumps. Others prefer to add the filler to the glue

very slowly without stirring, letting the filler sink to the bottom of the pot and build up until it has nearly reached the level of the liquid that is absorbing it. Then they stir the mixture very carefully, just enough to ensure even consistency throughout, and strain it through cheesecloth. The advantage of the latter method is that it depends less upon stirring, which can create minute air bubbles that mar the smoothness of the gesso when it is applied to the panel.

While still warm, the gesso is brushed onto the panel with a wide flat bristle brush. It is best to work systematically, starting from one edge of the panel, with strokes that are parallel to the edge and to each other. This first coat should be slightly thinner than subsequent coats and almost scrubbed onto the surface. It should be uniform and free from any bubbles. As soon as it has dried to a dull matte — and is dry to the touch — the second coat is applied, with the brushstrokes running across (at a right angle to) the previous ones. Four to six coats are applied in this manner — as soon as the previous coat is dry, and with brushstrokes running across those of the previous coat.

The gesso must be kept at the proper consistency throughout. As it cools, it will begin to set. When this happens, put it over the double boiler again to reheat; stir it carefully and remove it from the heat as soon as the desired consistency is reached.

When the last coat of gesso is completely dry, sand the surface. Begin with a medium-grain sandpaper and finish with a fine grain to obtain an ivory-smooth finish. Fold the sandpaper around a block of wood so that uniform pressure is applied. Finally, wipe the gesso surface with a slightly dampened cloth or sponge to remove the fine particles left from sanding.

BRUSHES AND OTHER EQUIPMENT

Both sable and bristle brushes are commonly used in tempera painting. Sables are useful for small areas and detail work; bristles for laying in broad areas. Rounds are preferable to flats, and rounds with longer hairs (or bristles) are better for tempera work than those with shorter hairs, because they hold more color and feed it out smoothly.

Only the best quality brushes should be used, as with any medium. Ideally, you should have an assortment of sizes and, even more important, enough brushes to reserve each for one particular color. This will ensure that the various color areas stay clear and separate. If you use only one or two brushes, be sure to rinse them out thoroughly before use with each new color. And, of course, they must be cleaned well after each use. Tem-

The basic equipment for painting in tempera.

pera that dries in a brush becomes hard and quite insoluble. Further, if traces of paint are left around the
ferrule, the hairs will soon start breaking and the brush
will not point as it should.

Besides brushes, you will need a nonporous surface
on which to put out and mix your colors. A porcelain

palette, or simply a slab of glass, will serve.

For grinding the pigments, a palette knife, slab, and
muller are needed, as well as a number of small jars
with tight-fitting lids for storing the various pigment-
and-water pastes. A small jar is needed for the egg emulsion, another for water.

Andrew Wyeth used tempera on a gesso panel for his best-known painting, *Christina's World*. The medium was held in tight control; each tiny brush stroke is calculated and precise. The overall clarity takes this work beyond realism into the realm of "magic realism," seen in the dreamlike quality and overtones of barrenness and interminable silence.

AN APPROACH TO PAINTING WITH TEMPERA

Since tempera is a precise medium, generally a painting is carefully planned ahead of time. After the composition has been worked out in a series of preliminary sketches, the design is drawn on the gesso panel. Cennini recommended that the first drawing on the gesso be done in charcoal — a good idea because corrections can be made easily. The excess charcoal dust is lightly brushed away and, if the design is satisfactory, the faint lines that remain are redrawn with fine brush and ink.

According to Cennini, the painting process was begun with a monochromatic underpainting in green earth; the modern painter who wishes to work in traditional fashion can use this pigment. Eight or ten coats of thinned or transparent tempera colors were laid over

"Death of the Virgin," a small panel from the great *Maestà* altarpiece by Duccio (1278-1319). Tempera.

This energetic portrayal of *The Youthful David* was commissioned of Andrea del Castagno in the mid-fifteenth century. Since it was to be a parade shield, it was executed on leather.

Decorativeness and detailed naturalism are combined in the portrait at left, *Princess of the House of Este*, thought to be Ginevra d'Este, painted by Pisanello (1395-1455).

this to heighten the colors and model the forms, and modeling was further refined by cross-hatching with a fine brush.

Tempera should be well thinned with water, color and solidity of form being built up in even applications of several glazes rather than by the impasto technique. The thin coats will dry quickly, so they may be applied in rapid succession and painting can proceed without interruptions. Brush the paint on with a series of strokes, as you would shade an area with pencil. For the best effects, tempera should not be applied thick or in washes, nor should it be blended, or smoothed on like

oil or watercolor. Its special quality is achieved, rather by precise brushwork.

Tempera painting should be approached methodically, working from broad forms to fine details, from local colors to gradations and then to shadows and highlights, from flat tones to iridescence. Thus, the earliest stage of the painting should be done in colors of medium value and intensity, and the areas of darkest and lightest values and high-intensity colors are developed in the final stages. In Pisanello's *Portrait of Ginevra d'Este* the linear patterns of the brocade on the oversleeve were painted on after the folds had been completed.

OPVS·RAROLI·CRIVELLI·VENET·

This panel of *St. Mary Magdalen* has the characteristic touch of the Renaissance painter Carlo Crivelli (1430?-?1494), whose work is charged with a unique poetry, calligraphic vitality, and tactile charm.

Reginald Marsh (1898-1954) used egg tempera for a large number of his acrid paintings. In such works as *Twenty-Cent Movie*, painted in the mid 1930s, he captured the vividness and kaleidoscopic vulgarity of the American urban scene.

Although some artists prefer to leave the surface of their tempera paintings as is, most follow the tradition of applying a coat of varnish. Cennini advised the artist to take clear, light-colored *vernice liquida* (a varnish made from sandarac resin dissolved in linseed oil) and apply it with the hand or a sponge. This practice of varnishing was so usual in Cennini's day that *vernice liquida* was sold ready-made — probably the first material the artist did not have to laboriously prepare for himself.

Although Cennini specified light-colored varnish, varnish made from sandarac always has a slight reddish-brown tone. Therefore, Renaissance painters apparently "planned" its effect into their work. They left tonalities light enough to compensate for the slight darkening of the colors by the varnish, and the varnish served to unify the paintings.

The primary function of varnish, actually, is to protect the surface of the painting. The artistic consideration, which was important in Cennini's day, is less compelling to the modern painter — the varnishes avail-

able today are quite transparent and nearly colorless. Two equally satisfactory varnishes are available: mastic and dammar. Neither is perfect; which one you choose depends upon which assets you value most. Dammar is transparent and dries to a harder finish than mastic, but it has a faint yellowish tone and is somewhat difficult to brush on. A dammar-varnished surface has less tendency to bloom (that is, to develop a whitish blotching caused by a condensation of moisture between the surface of the painting and the varnish). On the other hand, mastic is easier to remove when a painting is to be varnished anew. Whichever you use, purchase only the highest quality varnish, prepared exclusively for the artist. Commercial versions contain ingredients that may darken the painting or react adversely with the pigments.

The methodical approach outlined here *is* demanding — but tempera has already been described as a demanding medium. Yet — perhaps because of the challenge it presents — tempera, handled in its own terms, is one of the most rewarding of the painting media.

Contemporary with Marsh yet worlds removed from him is Mark Tobey, a painter whose work reflects his deep affinity with Zen mysticism. Turning tempera to inner, meditative expression, he has produced delicate and complex abstractions such as this, painted on a cardboard support, entitled *New Life*.

Subway Reading by Isabel Bishop is a twentieth-century example of a painting done in tempera and oils.

Oil paint is a remarkably flexible medium. From its inception in the early fifteenth century to our own time, its range has encompassed diverse expressions, as illustrated by examples reproduced here. The panel at left, depicting St. Joseph, is a detail from the *Merode Altarpiece* probably by Robert Campin (1375-1444.) *The Table*, right, was painted by Georges Braque (1882-1963).

114

INTRODUCING OIL PAINTS

The oil medium is remarkable for both its youth and the rapidity with which it supplanted all of the venerable, custom-sanctioned media. Within a few decades it became almost the universal vehicle of expression in Western painting. Artists of the Renaissance laid aside tempera and fresco for oil paints, and until recently most artists followed suit. Painting and oil painting are, at least in the popular conception, almost synonymous, because nearly all of the familiar paintings *are* oils — the Raphaels, Titians, Rembrandts, Vermeers, Goyas, van Goghs, Picassos, and so on.

The medium that took the Renaissance by storm has rather obscure beginnings. It is convenient to say that the van Eyck brothers invented it, and we have eloquent testimony of its earliest consummate use in the *Ghent Altarpiece*, which was commissioned of Hubert and finished by Jan (Hubert died in 1462, midway through the project). The truth is, of course, that the Flemish brothers did not invent — or suddenly hit upon — the oil medium, but rather developed a way of handling it that dramatically expanded the potentialities of painting.

Theophilus, in the twelfth century, mentioned the use of oil in painting. However, not until artists strove to describe the material world in minute detail and to render sun-bathed expanses of atmosphere could the special qualities of oils be "discovered" — that is, fully appreciated. It was the van Eycks who put oil glazes to work in this way, and the near-magical effects they achieved left other artists no option but to learn the secret and the technique. Thus, the medium was almost universally adopted in Europe, first by northern painters and then by Italian artists, in the fifteenth century.

The meticulous van Eyck glazes were soon exchanged for an increasingly direct, or *alla prima*, application of the pigments, but the medium itself remained at the forefront. Perhaps the very flexibility of oil paints accounts for their continuing popularity. The medium embraces extremes. Some artists work slowly and gradually, using painstakingly built-up glazes, as in the

8.

Oil Paints

Banker and His Wife, by Quentin Massys (1466?-1530), illustrates the indirect use of oils. The painting was built up with a series of layers of scumbles and glazes. At each stage the paint was thinly applied, and the brushstrokes were smoothed and blended.

Merode altarpiece probably painted by Robert Campin and Quentin Massys' *Banker and His Wife.* The van Eycks, El Greco, Rouault, and Klee were masters of this approach. Other artists work directly, laying on buttery paint in thick impasto. This approach is seen in the paintings of Frans Hals, Pierre Soulages, and Vincent van Gogh. The Campin altarpiece (page 114) and van Gogh's *Sunflowers* (opposite) are painted with totally different techniques and sum up reality in totally different ways. Yet both are oil paintings, and the differences

between them serve to illustrate the remarkable expressive range and versatility of the medium. Between these two techniques — the indirect and the direct (*alla prima*) — lie many intermediate possibilities. So great a versatility implies that there is no single "correct" technique for using oils, and this is true.

Some people spend years learning about oils and their use. Others simply buy some tubes of paint and brushes and set to work. Artists with little or no training can use the medium with great success, concentrating entirely

116

on what they have to say — as does the true "primitive." The sparkling, delightful New England scenes by Grandma Moses and Joseph Gatto's remarkable paintings (see page 44) prove the point: it is possible to simply take up brushes and oils and start painting. Whether the introduction to the medium is formal or casual, the association that follows is apt to be long and satisfying.

Sunflowers, by Vincent van Gogh, demonstrates the direct or *alla prima* technique. The paint was mixed and applied without modification, creating a rich, highly textured impasto surface.

PALETTE

As a glance at any art-store display will attest, you can buy a great number of oil colors. There is no need to invest in all of them; in fact, it is better not to. Instead, you should select a few from the bewildering array. This immediately brings up the question, "Which ones?" There is no recommended list, so the selection may be based on personal preference. However, some suggestions may be helpful. Two varieties of oil paints are available: they are labeled "student" and "artist." Student colors are not as high in quality, but they are considerably less expensive than artist colors and quite adequate for a beginner. It is a good idea for the beginner to start with a few colors, perhaps just one or two permanent ones from each of the color groups. Among the dependable pigments are the alizarin and Mars colors; the red and yellow oxides; strontium yellow, barium yellow, and Naples yellow; the siennas and umbers; cobalt blue, green, and violet; ultramarine blue and cerulean blue; viridian and chromium-oxide green; zinc, flake, and titanium-oxide white; carbon and ivory black, and lampblack.

Several pigments have a tendency to darken, and you should take this into consideration when using them. Among them are the alizarin blues and greens (some of the alizarin reds deepen slightly), and vermilion. Others — such as flake white and Naples yellow — darken when mixed with certain other pigments.

Some of the colors in the oil palette are more opaque than others. Among the more opaque colors are red oxide, the cadmium and chrome colors, ocher, barium yellow, and cobalt green. Among the more transparent are the alizarin colors, strontium yellow, cobalt blue, green earth, and viridian, and these may be used for glazes.

The chrome oranges, reds, and yellows are all right for studies and sketches, but they are not permanent and should be replaced by the more expensive cadmium colors for paintings that are intended to last.

A number of valuable oil colors are poisonous: the lead whites (flake white and Cremnitz white), emerald green, Naples yellow, chrome yellow, and cobalt violet. These should be kept out of reach of children and handled with reasonable care. Do not allow them to come in contact with any abrasions on the skin, and wash your hands carefully after using them. Do not use these pigments if you grind your own colors.

Take a commercially produced tube of oils, remove the cap, and squeeze out a dab of paint. It is smooth, glistening, and buttery. This paint was produced by thoroughly mixing the dry pigment with oil (ordinarily, linseed oil) — a long, exacting process involving mixing and mulling to disperse the pigment particles evenly.

Two other ingredients were probably also added in very small amounts, although they are not an essential part of oil paint: a stabilizer and a drier. The stabilizer, often beeswax, keeps the oil and pigment from separating; this is particularly important because the tubes of paint may lie for a long time in a warehouse or on a shop shelf before being used. As its name suggests, the drier (ordinarily a metallic salt) hastens the drying process. Different pigments dry at different rates, owing to a complex set of reactions between the pigment and the oil. For practical purposes, it has become accepted to even out the length of drying time to a uniform "average." This is done by speeding up the drying rate of some pigments and slowing down the rate of others; for instance, amounts of an oil that dries more slowly than linseed — e.g., poppyseed — may be added.

Pigments, of course, are the core of any painting medium, but oil is the substance that distinguishes oil paints from all others. Oil is, first, the vehicle in which particles of pigment are mixed and ground to produce the paint. When the paint has been applied, it is the oil that dries and acts as a binder, causing the pigments to adhere to the ground and creating a hard film that locks in and protects the pigment particles.

Oil may be added to the paint as it is being used if greater fluidity is desired. The oils used are the drying oils (linseed is the most common), which are also used in mixing the paint initially. Because the oil film has a tendency to yellow, using oil alone is not recommended. To achieve the desired fluidity in the paint and still keep the oil content at a minimum, you can combine the oil with dammar varnish and turpentine. Too much varnish invites cracking, and turpentine alone will cause the paint to run and bleed. But roughly equal parts of the oil and varnish to two parts of turpentine is a sound recipe, and small amounts may be used with the paint for impasto consistency, larger amounts for glazes.

SUPPORTS

Oil painting and canvas are inextricably linked, for this has been the major support used for the medium almost from the first. In fact, an oil painting done on a fabric support is referred to as a canvas. So the terms are firmly — and sometimes even mistakenly — linked. When used to refer to the support, "canvas" means a heavy textile of closely woven and relatively coarse fibers. The fibers may be jute, hemp, cotton, or flax. Only cotton or linen (the fabric woven from flax) should be used for permanent paintings, and of these two, linen is superior because it stretches, primes, and ages better than cotton

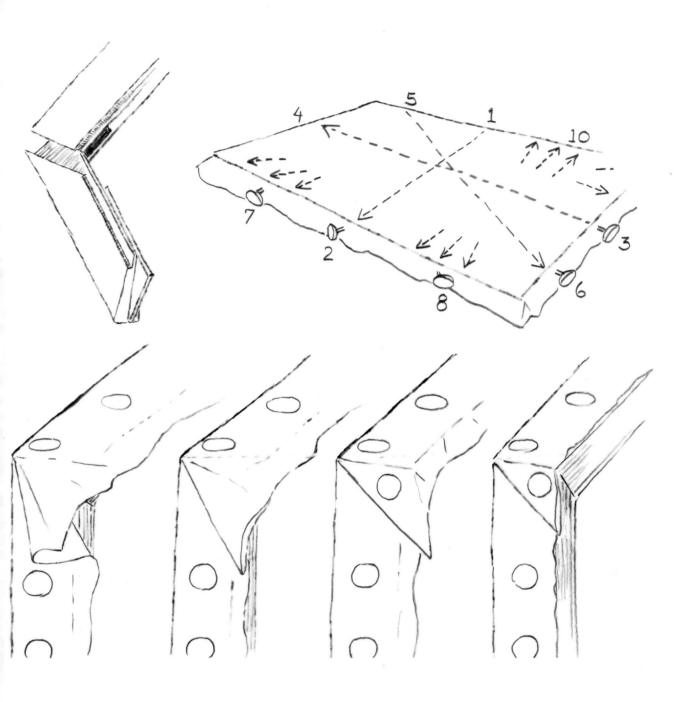

Top, left, corner section of stretcher bars showing the grooves that fit together for the mitered, mortised corners. Top, right, top view of canvas being stretched, showing the placement of the first few tacks and (by the directional arrows) the way the canvas is pulled taut before each tack is driven in. The sequence of four drawings shows one method of finishing the corners. The canvas is folded over in a square corner fold, a tack is driven into the heaviest wood of the tongue-and-groove joint, and the excess canvas is trimmed off along the back edge of the frame.

Senora Sabasa García, by Francisco de Goya (1746-1828).

and is less susceptible to atmospheric changes (cotton tends to expand and contract).

Canvas (that is to say, fabric) is by nature flexible, so it must somehow be made firm for painting. The early practice was to glue it to a wooden panel; now it is generally stretched over a frame.

Oil paint is not applied directly to the canvas because the pigments and oils cause unprotected fabric to rot. Thus, it is necessary to give the fabric a coating of glue size (made from animal hide) to seal the surface. Over the size, priming, which produces an even, white surface of uniform absorbency and texture, is applied. The priming is the ground on which the painting is executed. It is, in essence, the first coat of paint, and it is extremely important — it acts as a sort of shock-absorber between the support and the subsequent layers of pigment that form the actual painting.

You can purchase canvas that has already been stretched or glued to a cardboard or composition-board backing and sized and primed, or you can obtain it in rolls (sized and primed or raw) or piece by piece. The range of price is great, and corresponds to the quality of the canvas.

If you intend to do a great deal of painting, you might consider that it is far more economical to buy a whole roll of canvas rather than to buy it piece by piece. A roll of good sized and primed canvas costs no more than a comparable amount of inferior canvas bought a bit at a time. And if you are willing to size and prime the canvas yourself, you can buy raw linen, the finest canvas, which will be far superior to a comparably priced canvas that has been factory prepared.

The modern frame consists of wooden stretcher bars with mitered tongue-and-groove joints at the ends. These come in lengths ranging from about 6 inches to 6 feet. In purchasing them, be sure that they are of good, well-dried wood that will not warp.

To stretch prepared canvas, first put the four bars together. The rectangle must be true, with sides parallel and corners forming right angles. Then cut the canvas, adding to each dimension about 4 inches more than the actual size of the frame to allow for stretching the canvas over the edges of the frame. (For example, if the frame is 24 by 48 inches, the rectangle of cut canvas should be 28 by 52 inches.)

Place the canvas face down on a flat surface and center the frame on it. The weave of the canvas should be parallel with the sides of the frame. (If it is not, move the frame slightly, so that the weave and frame align.) Two inches of canvas will extend beyond the frame on each of the four sides.

Next, tack the canvas to the frame. You will need carpet tacks, a hammer, and canvas-stretching pliers.

(Upholsterers' pliers work equally well. A pair of ordinary carpenters' pliers can be substituted if you use them carefully; they have a very narrow grip and will rip the canvas if force is exerted hastily in the tightening process. But the canvas cannot be quite so tautly stretched as with the proper canvas-stretching pliers.) To begin, bring up the overlap on one of the shorter sides and tack it to the center of the outside edge of the frame. Drive in the tack only about one-half of its length — just enough to hold the canvas firmly to the edge. Now pull the canvas firm by hand and lightly tack it at the center of the edge of the opposite side. Similarly tack the canvas on the third and fourth sides. At this point, the canvas is fixed to the frame with four tacks, one on each side.

Now drive in a tack (again only part-way) midway between each center tack and a corner of the frame, working as before, first on one side and then opposite. Before putting in each tack, pull the canvas as taut as possible by hand. Always exert the force away from the center of the canvas.

You now have three temporary tacks evenly spaced along each of the four edges of the canvas. If the canvas is small, these twelve tacks are probably sufficient for this initial stretching; otherwise, add a tack between each two in the same way. The temporary tacks should occur roughly every 4 to 6 inches up to the beginning of the joint grooves at each corner. Wrinkles will probably appear around the first four tacks and, as you proceed, around the other temporary tacks. However, working systematically, you now remove the temporary tacks one by one, pull the canvas tighter with the pliers, and drive the tacks in again, this time all the way. When you have finished, the canvas surface should be absolutely smooth and tight. Add more tacks, if necessary, so that finally they occur at 1½- to 2-inch intervals. Tighten the canvas with the pliers before each tack is driven in.

When the canvas is stretched tightly and permanently tacked on the four edges, the corners are finished. Fold the canvas over each corner and tack it down. The tongue-and-groove joints are made so that the surface of the wood is wider on one side of the groove than the other; drive the tacks at the corners into this heavier, more substantial part of the frame.

If there are any remaining wrinkles, remove the tacks nearby and tighten the canvas more. Trim off the excess canvas along the back edge of the stretcher bars with a mat knife or razor blade, or fold it onto the back surface of the stretchers and tack it down.

In a well-stretched canvas, the tension exerted along all four edges of the frame is equal, and the working surface is taut and utterly smooth. Eight small wooden wedges or "keys" come with each set of stretcher bars. These are used to further tighten the canvas if — or when — necessary. They are driven into the inside corners of the frame (two in each corner). What they do, in essence, is force the frame joints apart. They should not be used to tidy up — or cover up — a careless stretching job, but rather to take up slack that may appear during or after painting.

If you are going to size the canvas, stretch it evenly but not too tightly on the frame; drive the tacks half-way in all around the frame. Then dampen the canvas evenly with water, using a sponge or large brush. This causes the fibers to stretch, and then, in drying, tighten to the frame. When dry, re-tack the canvas, this time tightly and permanently.

The surface is now ready for the glue size. Prepare the size as described on page 106. When it has cooled slightly, brush it on the canvas. The coat should be even and just thick enough to sink into the fibers and pores, but not so thick that visible excess builds up on the surface.

When the size is dry, the priming is applied. This consists of a coat — preferably, two coats — of a thick white paint, usually a mixture of white lead ground to a paste in linseed oil. The paste should be thinned with turpentine just enough to make brushing it on the surface possible. Some artists use a spatula rather than a brush to apply the priming. Whichever is used, the paint should be spread uniformly and smoothly. As soon as the first coat is dry, the second should be applied. The ground must be allowed to dry thoroughly before it is painted upon. Since the paint will have worked into the interstices of the weave, it will take at least ten days to two weeks for the two coats to dry completely.

Besides canvas, which is so firmly associated with the medium, there are a number of supports that may also be used in oil painting. One is, of course, the wood panel, discussed in the section on tempera. Another is glass, which figured prominently in late medieval and early Renaissance experiments with staining; however, its nonporous surface provides little for paint to cling to. Sheet metal, too, has been used for oil painting. Small easel paintings were done on copper panels in Italy and even more frequently in northern Europe, especially in Holland in the sixteenth and seventeenth centuries. The surface was roughened with an abrasive so the paint would adhere. A number of such paintings have survived, indicating that metal makes a relatively strong and permanent support. However, the practice has virtually been abandoned, for good reasons. Copper is quite

soft and inclined to bend easily (thin sheets of any metal are susceptible to dents); iron and tin are apt to rust; aluminum reacts chemically with some paint pigments, and so on, one by one, metals are disqualified as really satisfactory supports for painting.

Leather, parchment, and vellum have been decorated with oils or have served as supports for oil paintings on occasion. The miniature *Portrait of a Young Man* by Holbein, reproduced on page 34, was done in oils on vellum.

Oddly enough, rag paper and cardboard if prepared properly make far better, more permanent supports than metals. For any works intended as more than rapid sketches the surface must be sealed with a coat or two of sizing. Otherwise, the paper (or cardboard) acts as a blotter, absorbing the oil and leaving on the surface an insubstantial film of pigment surrounded by a "halo" of oil.

BRUSHES AND OTHER EQUIPMENT

Oil painting is done with brushes — bristle and sable — and palette knives. Bristle brushes are most commonly used, and all of them — flat, bright, and round — are particularly suited to oil painting. Being stiff, they leave ridges and textured patterns in the thick paint and give each brushstroke the tactile quality that is characteristic of the medium.

Palette knives also produce a tactile effect, and some artists use them almost exclusively. Both the flexible, tapered painting knife as well as the broad-bladed palette knife may be used. With the knife edge you can "incise" a layer of pigment to achieve a serrated effect or curving, swirling, or pointillist strokes. The effects that can be achieved with a palette knife are similar to those of the bristle brush but sharper, with a clearer definition of stroke.

Sable brushes may also be used in oil-painting — flat ones for smoothing strokes and painting details, round ones for narrow lines and fine details. If you use sables exclusively for an oil painting, the effect will be entirely different than with bristles and palette knives. Sables are soft, and they blend and smooth the colors. To paint with the most flexible sables, the pigments must be thinned considerably. Therefore, transitions between color passages tend to be gradual, and the individual strokes are minimized. For some purposes this use of the medium may be acceptable, but in general the bristle brush and palette knife are more direct and expressive of the qualities of oils.

The palette used for paints has changed little over the past several hundred years. It is oval or rectangular, traditionally made of wood, with a hole through which the

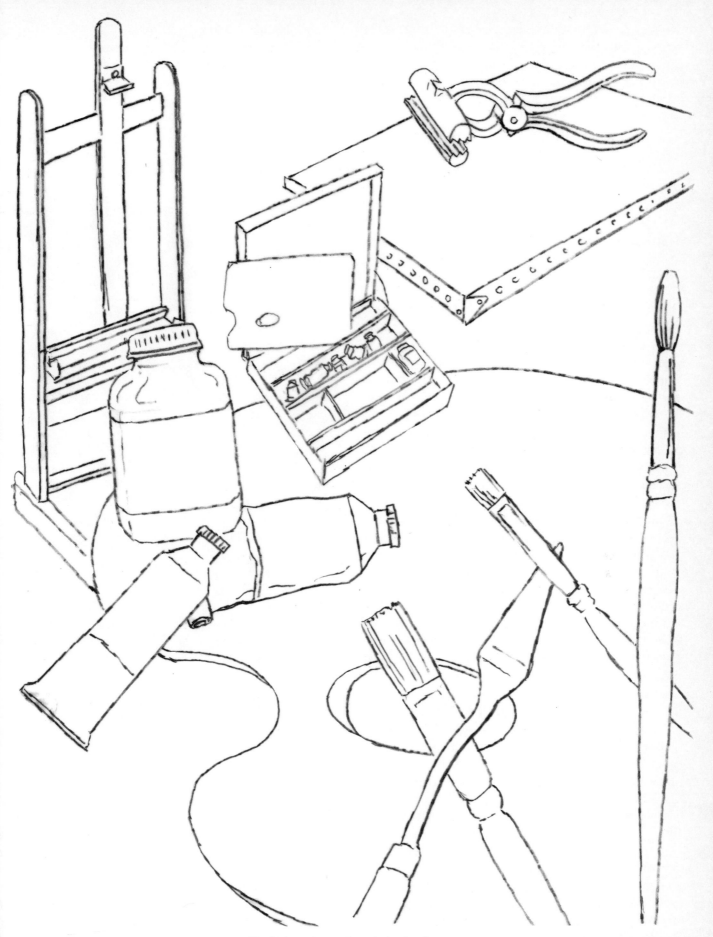

The basic equipment for painting in oils.

thumb is inserted so that it may be easily held. The palette cups, usually about the size of jigger glasses, clip on to the palette, and hold small amounts of linseed oil, turpentine, or the binder mixture. Larger amounts of binder may be kept at hand in jars.

Many artists substitute plastic or china plates, slabs of glass, or other hard, nonporous surfaces for the traditional palette. These surfaces are somewhat easier to clean — dried pigment is scraped off with a razor blade. Since it is more awkward to hold a plate or similar palette, having a small table at one's elbow on which to put it is a necessity. The palette you choose is entirely a matter of personal preference. All you need, basically, is some surface to hold the paint and containers of some kind for oil and turpentine.

AN APPROACH TO PAINTING WITH OILS

With oils, it is possible to take up paints and brush and simply start to paint, and this direct approach no doubt sounds like the simplest one. Certainly it is for some. But it requires you to have the finished painting firmly in mind at the outset, and then to methodically arrive at it, with each stroke final as it is made. As suggested at the beginning of this chapter, there are many and varied possible ways to handle oils. The approach outlined here is not unusual: it is a good introduction to the medium because it makes use of a number of direct and indirect techniques.

Begin the work with a monochrome sketch or underpainting in which the basic forms and composition are established. The color may be umber or sienna or any of the relatively subdued pigments that will not get in the way of later color development. At first, thin the paint down greatly with the oil-varnish-turpentine mixture and use free, sketchy strokes; then, with heavier color, firm up the faint lines with accenting strokes and lines. When the sketch is dry, you can scrub on the thinned pigment with a large flat or bright bristle brush, laying a light film of color over broad areas and passages of the composition to give it an overall tonal effect. A similar effect can be achieved by rubbing on unthinned pigment with a cloth or the fingers; excess paint may be rubbed off with the cloth. At this point, you will be able to see a loose, shadowy version of what the finished work will be taking shape in the broad areas of light and dark and in the sketchy lines of various weights and density.

When the initial underpainting is dry, introduce the broad color areas. These too will constitute underpainting — they will not be seen in the finished work. The function of these colors is to provide cool or warm tones on which to lay later applications of paint. If they are opposite, or complementary, tones, they will increase the luminosity and subtlety of the final colors. For example, underpainting for flesh tones may be blue, and for blue drapery, red. Apply these tones thinly and loosely, so that the effect is rather like a subdued watercolor. The tones should work with the initial underpainting, defining the composition and heightening the forms.

In Leonardo's unfinished *St. Jerome*, the dark areas have been blocked in. Glazes and scumbles that build up the forms can be seen; there is light scumbling, for instance, on the shoulder area. Only the saint's head, neck, and right shoulder were brought anywhere near completion; everything else on the panel is underpainting.

When dry, the areas of color may be modified by glazes and scumbles. In his unfinished *St. Jerome*, Leonardo introduced scumbled highlights over the glazes in the shoulder, neck, and head of the figure. Leonardo began his painting on a light ground; when the ground is dark, as in the unfinished *Angel of the Annunciation* by Tintoretto, initial laying in of broad forms may be done in a scumble. The right hand and arm and drapery of the figure were painted in this way.

Abraham Rattner used compartmentalized areas of color on a dark ground to suggest the impact and brilliance of stained glass in *The Emperor* (above). His painting is a scathing indictment of power, which "pollutes whate'er it touches."

Until the sixteenth century, canvases were given a light ground; then, many artists began to use dark grounds, particularly for very large paintings. Not only did this speed up work because the dark ground functioned as part of the finished painting; but, as may be seen in the *Angel of the Annunciation* (right) by Tintoretto (1518-1594), the dark ground also set off more effectively brilliant flashes of color and dramatic highlights and invited rapid, broad, direct brushwork.

So far you have worked indirectly, with each layer building upon and modifying the previous ones but not obscuring them as the painting "emerges." You can finish the painting completely in this way, but the final stages are now generally completed in direct painting. Brushstrokes of opaque or semi-opaque pigment are laid on. Work over the entire picture area with each color so that the whole is at the same stage of development at any given moment. Apply broad areas of local color first, and gradually build up the passages of more intense color, darker notes, and lights. You may use

With every brushstroke in *Still Life with Cherries and Peaches* (right), Paul Cézanne (1839-1906) pursued the structure and inter-relation of forms. In *The Liver Is the Cock's Comb* (below) by Arshile Gorky, the freely invented organic shapes and ambiguous images are mythlike — a poetic vision of creation and primordial energy.

impasto, applying the paint so thickly that the forms are actually raised above the surface of the painting. The rich effect of this technique may be seen in van Gogh's *Sunflowers* (page 117).

In general, transitions between color areas are better accomplished by using transitional tones than by blending adjacent colors. If the colors are mixed on the canvas, they may be muddied and lose their strength and brilliance. Too much elaboration and finicky detail will weaken the effect of direct oil painting. Think of yourself as painting from a distance: let the colors work side by side and let broad, "coarse" brushstrokes stand. Back away from the canvas repeatedly to see if the painting "holds up."

You should make each stroke as though it were final, and not work over or worry it. Such structural brushwork should be broad and so calculated that it defines the forms, as is superbly illustrated in Goya's *Señora Sabasa García* (page 120), Cézanne's *Still Life with Cherries and Peaches,* Pierre Soulages' *4 July 1956,* and Willem de Kooning's *Woman in Landscape IV* (reproduced on page 39).

Broad, insistent brushstrokes explore the sensuous qualities of the paint and convey the energy and excitement of the act of painting in *4 July 1956* by Pierre Soulages.

127

As in the still life on page 126, Cézanne's major concern in *The Poorhouse on the Hill* (above) was the structure of the composition; the subject matter is of secondary importance. The contemporary artist Balcomb Greene similarly emphasized the internal structure of his *Rocks on the Edge of the Sea* (opposite), a tight-knit work of precisely rendered interlocking areas.

Muse was painted by Robert Gwathmey in 1966. The work's appealing decorative style contains the barb of social comment, reflecting the artist's one continuing major theme — the injustice and alienation imposed by segregation.

128

129

To pop-art fare, Wayne Thiebaud has almost literally contributed the dessert course. He used the delicate, chalky quality of pastels to advantage in this paean to pastry entitled *Cakes #1.*

INTRODUCTION TO PASTELS

Pastel painting was the child of eighteenth-century courtly French sensibilities. The exquisitely refined, delicate tone, the very fragility of the medium itself, expressed better than any other the quality of that wan, hyper-refined age. Pastels actually had made their first appearance more than a century earlier, but the beginnings of the medium are obscure. Lomazzo, a sixteenth-century Italian writer, attributed the invention of pastels to Leonardo da Vinci. More likely, they were the invention of Leonardo's followers, inspired by his use of red chalk. (It is said that Leonardo probably was the first artist to use this medium.) Once the idea of one color in stick form was born — or rather, when a colored chalk was added to the white chalk and black charcoal long in use — it was but a short step to a whole range of colors. By the mid-seventeenth century, pastels were relatively common.

Pastels nevertheless "belong" to the eighteenth century. Maurice Quentin de La Tour, an irascible painter in the court of Louis XIV, was the first to use them, superbly and virtually exclusively, as a major medium. A number of his contemporaries used them too, the best known being Jean Baptiste Perroneau and Chardin. Chardin painted in oils most of his life. Then, quite suddenly, he put down the brush and took up pastels, explaining that his infirmities made working in oils difficult: "For this reason," he wrote, "I have begun to work in pastels." The portraits and self-portraits he produced in his last years are among the finest examples of the medium.

Delacroix, the explosive romanticist, used pastels principally in studies for oil paintings. His sketches have a swirling freedom and are far removed from de La Tour's suavely precise and elegantly finished portraits. Manet, Renoir, Degas, and other late-nineteenth-century masters used pastels. Degas said he preferred pastels to any other medium for their brilliance and the

9.

Pastels

The fashionable eighteenth-century portraitist Maurice Quentin de la Tour used pastels almost exclusively for his later works. At left is his *Portrait de d'Alembert*; below, left, an unfinished portrait that illustrates how the features were expressively indicated at the outset in a few concise strokes.

rough, tense linear effect he could achieve even when laying in a solid color area. Mary Cassatt, the American turned Parisian, frequently used pastels in her charming pictures of women and children. Nor have modern painters overlooked the possibilities of pastels: the medium has been utilized by Odilon Redon, André Masson, Chagall, and Picasso, to name a few.

In pastel painting the pigments are held in the hand and applied directly to the support. One advantage of this medium is that it requires less equipment and fuss than any other — the only essentials are pastels and paper. In simple terms, pastels are dry pigments pressed into sticks, with a small amount of binding medium (usually gum tragacanth) to hold the finely ground particles together. The particles are bound firmly enough to hold the pressed form, but when the stick is drawn across the paper, a layer of the pigment dust sloughs off and is caught by the surface texture of the paper. The effect of the pigments is entirely pure in the deepest shades; in the lighter values it is modified to varying degrees depending upon the amount of precipitated chalk added in manufacture.

To achieve the best results with pastels, as with any medium, you should know its own special qualities. In all other painting media, the pigments are mixed with a binder and some liquid vehicle, and to a certain extent this alters the original intensity and quality of the colors. Pastel color is the pure, vibrant color of the pig-

The sensibilities and art of Chardin (1699-1779) ran in deeper and more humble channels than that of his eighteenth-century rococo contemporaries. His pastel *Self-Portrait* makes no concession to fashionable lace frills or courtly gestures.

Eighteenth-century pastel portraits were delicately executed and smoothly blended, as may be seen in the suave *Portrait of Noverre* (below, left) by Jean Baptiste Perroneau. A century later, when Edouard Manet painted the delightful, rather startled *George Moore* (below, right) the execution was broader, more rapid and sketchy with but cursory blending.

133

ment and, unless a fixative is applied, it remains unchanged. Certainly, then, one of the irresistible charms of the medium is its clear, singing colors. It has, or can have, a delicacy that is peculiarly its own.

Another asset is that pastels are applied dry. Thus, you can see what you have done immediately; drying alters the effect of colors somewhat. In addition, the colors can be worked, smoothed, and blended with the fingers, making it possible to achieve a marvellous subtlety in gradations of tone.

Technically, pastels have other advantages. They may be applied directly on the support, which does not require special preparation (although you may elaborate if you wish). The colors are ready — and when you have finished, cleaning up involves no more than putting pastels and paper away.

THE PALETTE

The range of pigments available in pastel form is wide but not all-inclusive. Pastels are as permanent as the pigments from which they are made. None of the toxic pigments (see page 103) can be made into pastels, of course, since working with them would mean breathing in a certain amount of the dust.

SUPPORTS

Paper, the most common support in pastel painting, is not generally thought of as a very durable material. Nevertheless, it is extraordinarily permanent — if you use the right kind, handle your work with reasonable gentleness, and display or store it carefully.

Rag papers are the most durable. They are, as the name implies, made from rags — generally cotton or linen. Time has shown that rag paper is more stable, less given to discoloration and disintegration, than paper made from wood pulp. You can see this for yourself by comparing a year-old newspaper (newsprint is a wood-pulp paper) to a letter written on fine-quality rag stationery a decade ago. In a year, the newspaper has become yellow and brittle; it is on the verge of falling apart. After ten years, the sheet of stationery is virtually unchanged.

A great variety of good rag art papers specifically suited to pastels is available. Three main characteristics will determine which you choose, depending upon the effects you wish to achieve. These are surface texture, color, and weight. The surface texture ranges from very fine to quite coarse. For very delicate, detailed effects, you would select the smoothest texture. Tinted paper provides a background tone for your painting; the color is an integral part of the composition, and the paper should be selected with this in mind. Color and grain can also unite to create an added effect. If the paper has a highly textured surface and is white or a very light tone, a sparkling pointillism results. The pastels do not cover the surface smoothly, but leave tiny spots of white where the paper shows through.

To a great extent, the weight of the paper you select is a matter of personal preference. It is a good idea, however, to mount very lightweight paper before you begin to work.

You can, if you wish, elaborate on the paper that is commercially available. Although a great variety of tinted papers is produced, you may wish to prepare a special tint yourself. This is done with watercolor, as follows: Mount the sheet on a drawing board with strips of brown butcher's tape around the edges. The paper should be smaller than the board — at least 1½ or 2 inches of board should show on all sides. Dampen the entire surface of the paper evenly with water, using a sponge or a large watercolor wash brush. Place the board on a flat surface. Load the brush with diluted paint and make broad, sweeping parallel strokes across the surface. The brushstrokes should not show. When the paper is thoroughly dry, remove it from the board by cutting through the tape, along the edge of the paper, with a razor or mat knife.

You can also give a paper extra tooth, or texture. To do this, mount it; then brush it with gum water and sprinkle on finely ground pumice.

Although paper can be a durable support, it is fragile and in general should be affixed to a drawing board for working purposes, or permanently mounted on a cardboard backing. You may also paste it on canvas or linen, which can then be tacked to a stretcher frame.

To mount the paper on cardboard, dampen the back of the sheet with water, using a sponge or large soft brush. Blot dry a border of about ½ or ¾ inch on all four edges and apply glue (white glue is good for the purpose). Place the paper on the backing, smoothing it as you do so. Sponge off any excess glue that appears along the edges, and cover the paper with a weighted drawing board so that it will dry flat.

A finished pastel painting may also be mounted in this way, but you must take much greater care. Use a smooth, nonporous surface such as glass when you place the pastel face down to dampen it. Be sure the paper doesn't shift from side to side during the process. When you place it on the mount, hold it carefully by the edges and cover the painting with a piece of paper before you smooth it, so your hand does not touch the pastel surface

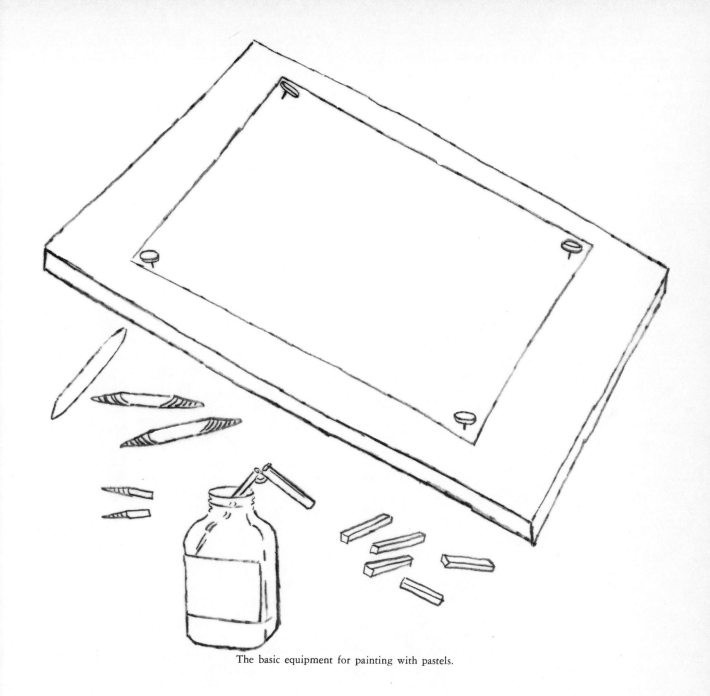

The basic equipment for painting with pastels.

EQUIPMENT

As noted in the introduction to pastels, the pigments are applied directly to the support. However, in addition to using the pastel stick itself and your fingers to achieve the effects you want, you can also use stiff bristle brushes to work the colors, or you may wish to use a stump. This is an implement used for smoothing or blending colors in various dry media, including pencil, crayon, and charcoal, as well as pastel. Stumps are made of relatively soft paper that is tightly rolled and pointed at one or both ends. (They have also been made of leather or felt, and leather ones are still manufactured.) Stumps come in various sizes. A special version is the tortillon: it is

made of harder paper, is pointed at only one end, and is only about 3 inches long.

How much you use stumps is a matter of preference — some artists do not use them at all, while others rely on them heavily. At least one artist, Mrs. Elizabeth Cay, an early nineteenth-century painter, actually applied pastels with stumps. Her box of pastels, (which is in the Victoria and Albert Museum in London) contains a set of leather stumps and bottles of pigment in powder form; the colors were apparently worked onto the paper by means of the stumps.

AN APPROACH TO PASTEL PAINTING

Pastel paintings may be done with or without preliminary sketching. However, if you sketch with any of the sketching crayons (such as conté crayon), your drawing should be worked out on a separate piece of paper and transferred to the working surface with lightly drawn pencil, chalk, or pastel lines, because pastel will not adhere to the crayon.

A few generalizations may be made about achieving the best results with pastels. In general, you should not plan to apply layer upon layer of color. Actually, the

Arthur Dove's paintings are among the first completely abstract works produced in this country; some date from as early as 1910. *Nature Symbolized, No. 2* translates natural elements into a lyrical pattern of color areas and curving shapes.

La Chanteuse Verte by Edgar Degas (1834-1917). Pastels on paper.

Animals Devouring Themselves by surrealist André Masson is a pointed reference to man's destructive nature.

medium does not lend itself to this technique. The tooth of the paper will only hold just so much pigment; if you apply more, it just falls off in fine dust. You can rub the surface after each application, which will smooth away the excess pigment and make room for more. This is all right if the overall brilliance of the pigments is not diminished by successive layers of color, but the effect is often muddy. Many artists apply a thin spray of fixative to the surface several times during the course of work, which prevents the particles of pigment from mixing. This procedure is valid so long as you realize that fixa-tive, even sparingly applied, affects the colors slightly and also modifies the texture of the pastels. However Edgar Degas apparently used this technique so that he could work over the surface again and again; only the finishing touches were put on with the pure colors which he left unfixed.

Blending, which creates subtle receding tones, is usu-ally done in the early stages of the work. When you have laid in these areas, the excess dust may be gently whisked off with a soft brush such as a camel hair o sable. Then, final details can be put on directly — tha is, without rubbing or blending the strokes. Working methods vary, of course. The amount of blending and smoothing and direct application employed differs from artist to artist and depends, too, on the effects desired.

De La Tour used blending and smoothing extensively. The result, as may be seen in any one of his countless portraits, is an astonishing realism. In his hands, pastels captured the images of powdered and wigged sitters better than any mirror would. Perroneau and Chardin had a more direct, unfused technique, allowing more of the strokes they drew to remain intact. Experimentation aside, however, the novice may keep the virtues of pastels in mind and be fairly sure of a satisfying result if the colors all remain clear and readable. Too much blending, even of colors that work together beautifully, produces an effect that is somehow too smooth and too mechanical, and at the same time saccharine. In general, the more direct and less contrived the working method, the better. Finicky touches, like over-working the color, are to be avoided — but this is true of every medium, not pastels alone.

Pastels can also be used in combination with other media. Perhaps the best way to briefly indicate the potential of pastels is to mention a few of the techniques employed by Degas, a master of the medium. Not only did Degas use pastels in the "traditional" fashion described above; he also combined them with gouache and tempera. Sometimes he also mixed powdered pastels with a liquid to make a sort of paste, which he then applied with a stiff brush. At other times he sprayed water on areas of pastel and spread the color with a brush, treating it somewhat like a wash. The variety of these approaches gives Degas' pastels an unparalleled richness, and his daring expanded the possibilities and flexibility of the pastel medium.

You will probably want at least occasionally to use a fixative. Fixatives are thin solutions of natural resins — dammar or mastic varnish or bleached shellac — in a fast-drying solvent such as alcohol (a slow-drying solvent would soak the particles of pigment, causing them to become dark and dull).

Fixative is sprayed on using either a spray can or an atomizer or mouth blower. The work to be sprayed is laid flat on a working surface. The fixative must be applied in a fine, even mist: test the flow before aiming it at the painting. Spray from about 12 or 16 inches above the pastel surface. Try to hold the nozzle just beyond the edges of the paper; if you hold it directly over the paper, drops that collect on the nozzle will fall onto the picture surface. Use a series of parallel sweeps back and forth across the painting to distribute the bands of fixative mist. Begin and end each sweep beyond the edges of the picture, and don't go over any part more than once — a second spraying will deposit too much fixative and change the color and texture of the pastel.

If you spray a finished pastel with fixative, it can be stored without difficulty, but you must still take care in handling the work, since fixative should be applied as sparingly as possible. The fixative will be dry by the time you have packed up your pastels, and the painting can be stored like any drawing — in a portfolio, large drawer, or other convenient place. However — and this is the one major drawback of the medium — no pastel that is really significant or of great importance to you should ever be sprayed with fixative. No matter how carefully done, the process does alter and coarsen the work. There are at least two ways to preserve a pastel painting that is not to be sprayed. One is to immediately frame it suitably. "Suitably" means there is a mat sufficiently thick to keep the pastel surface from touching the glass, and a frame that is backed to seal out dust and grime. Since pastel paintings cannot be dusted or washed, the necessity to do so must be avoided.

A painting may be stored unframed if utmost care is taken that nothing rubs across its surface. Several may be piled up, if a protective sheet is placed between each one and the next. The sheet must have a smooth, non-absorbent surface: highly coated (glossy) paper, cellophane, or sheet plastic (which has the advantage of firmness) will serve. If you wish to carry several pastels with you in a presentation portfolio, put each one in a folder of tagboard and plastic hinged together at the top with tape.

Op artists of the 1960s combined the scientific principles of optics, the precision of linear draftsman-ship, and the brilliance of new synthetic paints to create patterns that seem to shift and pulsate. This sensation results from the interaction between the work and the spectator's vision. Illustrated is Richard Anuszkiewicz's *Enshrined*, painted in Liquitex.

We come now to the last section of this account of media and techniques. The traditional media — watercolor, fresco, encaustic, tempera, and pastels — and the historical uses of art from which they developed have been examined. The final chapter presents a distinctly modern painting medium and touches upon the startling and unorthodox directions taken by modern art that makes use of a whole new vocabulary of materials and methods.

We have seen that the discovery and development of painting materials and methods goes hand in hand with the cultural intention — the artist speaks for his time, using the vocabulary that best expresses what he has to say. The technological age presents its own set of values and images — new realities — and has provided new means of expression for the artist. Of course, the traditional equipment is still at hand, and it is flexible enough to express a great deal, both old and new. Jackson Pollock used oils — much thinned, and sometimes dripped and flowed onto his canvases through perforated paint cans in "unorthodox" fashion — and Jasper Johns's pop-art flags and targets were done in encaustic. The point is that we have at our disposal virtually every medium and technique ever used in the past and, in addition, the modern synthetic media, which offer a range that has already proved remarkable and has not yet been fully explored.

NEW TECHNIQUES, NEW DIRECTIONS

The Sob, by David Alfaro Siqueiros, was painted in 1939 in Duco, (a cellulose-base lacquer and one of the early commercial synthetic paints), on composition board.

142

José Clemente Orozco once said, "Isn't it a pity that nothing has been done for the painter to save him time and energy, absolutely nothing, to enrich his palette or protect his creations against the ravages of the years!" These words were spoken in the early thirties; in the fifteen years that followed, another Mexican artist, José Gutiérrez, devoted himself to the problem, experimenting with plastics. Working with Jiménez Rueda at the National Polytechnic Institute in Mexico City, he developed such synthetics as Vinylite, pyroxylin, and ethyl-silicate compound — new materials, equally suited to easel painting and murals.

David Alfaro Siqueiros, one of the first artists to champion synthetics, wrote of Gutiérrez's achievement: "He has broken the single-technique control of traditional painting that dominates not only the academic but the pseudo-modern snob approach, by accumulating different easy modern processes of combining pyroxylin and Vinylite. Moreover, he adds to his techniques metallic elements creating new effects, such as glass and mirrors. He combines opaque and brilliant materials, the smooth and the rough, with equal success. In this way, he has enormously enriched the textural feeling of his entire work."

Even during the early experimental stages, Siqueiros used the synthetics — and did some experimenting on his own. In 1935 he established the Siqueiros Experimental Workshop in New York, and there he concentrated on improving the techniques of using synthetics.

Plastics were used first less than fifty years ago — in items such as combs and toothbrush handles; now they are a basic material in almost every field of endeavor — industry, commerce, science — and art. According to one report, a third of the artists in the United States have turned to the synthetic media. Among them are such

10.

Synthetic Paints

On the Wharf by Russell Woody. Politec on Masonite.

COURTESY, PACE GALLERY. PHOTOGRAPH, FERDINAND BOESCH

Nicholas Krushenick is an exponent of "new
abstraction," characterized by disarmingly simple flat designs, pure and evenly applied color,
and quasi-geometric shapes. To these qualities
Krushenick adds a refreshing touch of humor
in his *Elephant Spoons*, a work in acrylic on
canvas.

major painters as Hyman Bloom, Elaine de Kooning,
and Robert Motherwell, as well as many outstanding
illustrators, including the late Boris Artzybasheff, Aus-
tin Briggs, and Robert Weaver.

The synthetic paints are products of the chemical
laboratory and the test tube. The acrylic and vinyl resins
from which they are made are polymerized: polymerization is a chemical process that unites two or more
molecules of the same kind, changing a compound into
a new form, which has the same elements in the same
proportions but is composed of larger molecules with
a higher molecular weight. The new form has different
physical properties; thus, although the original compound may have been a volatile liquid, after polymerization it may be a nonvolatile, stable, elastic solid.

The synthetic resins may be used in an emulsion (minute particles of the resin are suspended in water) or in
a solution (the resins are dissolved in an organic solvent
such as acetone). Acrylic resins, in emulsions, are by far
the most widely used synthetic paints.

Polymer emulsions, as they are often called, have a
versatility that extends beyond painting — they are used
in sculpture and the graphic arts. Yet in painting alone
their versatility is remarkable; it has often been said
that the effects of every traditional medium can be ap-
proximated with polymer paints. It is possible to produce a thin glaze or a thick impasto, a glossy finish or
a matte finish — or any degree between — as well as
unique effects that cannot be achieved with any other
medium. (The polymers can, moreover, be used with
watercolor, gouache, casein, tempera, and — to some
extent — oils.)

When polymer emulsion dries, the paint film is tough
and durable. Although essentially a water-base paint
(water is used in the process of polymerization and is
the thinner for the paint), the resulting film is insoluble
in water — once dry, it cannot be redissolved. Each coat
of paint bonds with the paint beneath it to form one
continuous film, rather than separate, superimposed layers, as is the case with oils. The film is highly elastic;
that is, it expands and contracts as a unit without cracking — again unlike oils, in which the expansion and

David Hockney used acrylics for his scenery-laden *Portrait of Nick Wilder*. Current figurative and nonfigurative painting alike turn synthetics to a distinctly contemporary expression.

contraction of one of the lower layers may crack or craze the surface. Polymer-emulsion paint is not affected by light, heat, cold, or climatic changes, and it has great adhesive quality, binding firmly to the support. (The synthetic resins in general produce superior glues, such as white glue, which is vinyl resin.) The emulsion has a milky, opaque appearance but dries colorless and transparent; it does not alter the color of the pigments or yellow or darken with age. Finally, because it is water-based, polymer-emulsion paint dries quickly, which allows for great speed and variety of handling and control.

PALETTE

Most of the pigments associated with oils are also found in polymer emulsions — the exceptions are viridian and alizarin crimson. However, there are a number of synthetic pigments that not only replace these colors but also expand the synthetic-paint palette.

The number of colors available varies from brand to brand. In the Liquitex line there are some thirty colors, including a number of synthetic pigments such as Azo yellow, Napthol crimson, and Acra red. Politec, which was developed by José Gutiérrez and has been produced commercially for over a decade, is similar to Liquitex, but has a few less colors. Two brands that have appeared more recently, Aqua-Tec and Shiva Acrylic Colors, offer thirty-three colors; both are still being improved technically. The Shiva Acrylic Colors were developed particularly to resemble oil paints in handling and effect; as were the New Masters paints, which offer twenty-seven colors. A newer synthetic, Hyplar, is available in thirty-two colors. Liquitex and Aqua-Tec come in both jars and tubes; Politec and Hyplar in jars only, and Shiva Acrylic Colors and New Masters in tubes only. The jar colors have a thick liquid consistency, and the tube colors have a heavy body, like oil paint.

SYNTHETIC "VARNISH," MODELING PASTE, AND PRIMER

Most manufacturers of synthetic paints make polymer "varnishes" that may be mixed with or painted over the emulsions to obtain a matte or glossy finish. The Liquitex products are called Polymer Medium (for a glossy finish) and Matte Medium. The Politec paints dry to an opaque, matte finish; Barnis Sallador varnish is added to the colors for a medium gloss, and Luzitron for high gloss. The New Masters, Shiva, and Aqua-Tec lines include matte and gloss mediums.

Liquitex and Hyplar also carry gels, which are mixed with colors to give them greater body for impasto work.

Another product, modeling paste (or extender, as it

is sometimes called), serves a similar purpose as the gels, but has a far wider range of uses. This putty-like substance is made of polymer medium and marble dust and may be mixed with the paints as an extender; it gives them body and may be used to build up impasto areas. (It is also used as a material for sculpture.) Liquitex, Politec, Aqua-Tec, Shiva, and Hyplar all make modeling pastes.

A synthetic primer has also been developed. Most companies call their product "gesso," but this is inaccurate; do not use synthetic gesso if you want the traditional characteristics of gesso. Synthetic primer is excellent for preparing supports for polymer paintings, and it can be employed with the traditional media if you want to take advantage of its particular qualities — for example, its nonabsorbent finish. It is a bright white, rapid-drying liquid that may be applied thinly or relatively thickly, even on flexible supports, because of its pliancy.

SUPPORTS

Polymer paints may be used on virtually every clean, non-oily, porous support — including all the traditional supports, such as fabric, paper, wood, fiberboard, and walls. However, it is not necessary to prepare some of these supports in the traditional fashion. Fabric, for example, need not be sized and primed as for oil painting, because the synthetic paints themselves seal and protect the fibers. Only particularly absorbent fabrics really need to be primed to prevent the water in the emulsion from being absorbed too quickly and allow time for the film that holds the pigments to form. Canvases sized and primed for oil painting ordinarily should not be used for painting with synthetics because the linseed oil in the priming coats interferes with the formation of the film.

All varieties of paper — from fine illustration board to tissue — can be used. Mount the more fragile or flimsy papers on a substantial backing, such as tag board.

Panels may be primed with synthetic gesso. For a smooth ground, thin the gesso with one part water to three or four parts gesso and brush on three or four coats, running the brushstrokes in each coat at a right angle to those in the previous coat. The gesso may be used as is, producing a bright white ground, or it may be tinted with polymer colors before application to the support. Inert aggregates, such as sand, can be mixed with the gesso to create textural effects.

Polymer paints may be applied directly onto masonry or plaster walls (since the acrylics are alkaline, they are

The basic equipment for painting with synthetics.

unaffected by the alkaline content of plaster or cement). The paint does not sink in, but adheres to the surface. As with fresco work, however, it is best to erect a false wall in front of the structural wall. It may be constructed as described in the chapter on fresco painting (page 78) or consist of Masonite panels. Seal the backs of the panels with a coat of polymer paint, then glue and screw them to a wood frame. The faces of the panels may be primed with one or more coats of synthetic gesso. If you prefer a fabric texture, cover the panels with canvas. Glue it to the Masonite with polymer medium and prime it with at least one coat of polymer paint or synthetic gesso. The panels of a large mural may be installed and then painted or completed in the studio and then placed in position.

When selecting a support for work with synthetics, keep in mind these basic requirements: it should be porous (polymer paint film does not form a bond with nonporous surfaces such as glass), and it should not be oily or greasy. If the surface is especially hard and shiny, as is the smooth side of tempered Masonite, give it a slight tooth by sanding. If you are not certain whether to use a particular support, paint a test swatch, let it dry, and then wet it with water. If the paint adheres and resists being peeled or rubbed off, the support is satisfactory.

BRUSHES AND OTHER EQUIPMENT

All kinds of bristle and hair brushes can be used with the synthetics, and your selection will depend upon the effect you want to achieve. Ordinary, inexpensive brushes with nylon bristles also may be used. These are not recommended for any of the traditional media because they simply do not respond to the properties of these media. But they do seem "attuned" to the synthetic paints, which are themselves a form of plastic.

Do not allow synthetic paint to dry in the brushes, since it becomes insoluble. Even during a. painting session, you should thoroughly rinse out brushes not in immediate use before the paint can dry in the bristles. (If your brushes have plastic bristles, you can leave them immersed in a container of water without ill effect.) Then, after painting, clean all your brushes with water and a little soap and rinse them thoroughly.

You may also want to have painting and palette knives, which are useful for applying and building up areas of paint on the support as well as scraping the palette clean.

The most satisfactory palette is one of the several types used with other water-based media: a plate, porcelain palette, or slab of plate glass will work quite well. Paints put out on the palette will dry relatively quickly.

If the dabs dry before they are used, scrape them off before laying fresh paint on the palette — if the fresh paint is added over dried paint, bits of the dried paint film will lift up and mix into the new paint. Large amounts of a color may be mixed on the palette and stored in a covered jar. A film or skin will form on the top, but when you remove it, the paint beneath is usable.

Aside from brushes, palette, and, perhaps, a few jars, the only other necessity in terms of equipment is a water container. Or rather, two or three water containers — the water in a single container muddies quickly. This way, brushes can be rinsed initially in the first, again in the second, and finally in the third; the last will remain clean enough, during a session of several hours, for mixing with the paints.

SOME APPROACHES TO POLYMER PAINTING

Since the synthetic paints have a virtually limitless range, the possibilities outlined here form only an introduction. Other techniques may be uncovered by experimentation and study; if you want a complete course in the use of synthetics, the Bibliography includes a fine and definitive book, *Painting With Synthetic Media*, by Russell O. Woody.

When the more transparent of the synthetic paints are simply thinned with water, they are very much like watercolor, and the traditional watercolor brushwork and washes may be used, with the same effects. However, watercolor cannot be overpainted, except with the greatest care, because subsequent applications of paint redissolve what has previously been painted and may cause unintended bleeding and muddying of the colors. Synthetic paint, on the other hand, dries as quickly as watercolor, but becomes insoluble. Thus, no amount or kind of overpainting — washes, detailed brushwork, and the like — will alter the underlying work once it is dry. Corrections may be made, however: unsatisfactory areas are painted out with titanium white and then repainted.

When used like watercolor, polymer paints still form their characteristic film. For this reason, you cannot dilute them excessively with water; when extended too far, the pigments are not bound into the film. At a certain point, the pigments separate — a sort of "breaking apart" that is readily visible. If this happens, add a little matte medium to the paint. This will not affect the appearance of the wash; it simply binds the pigments.

The paints can be diluted and used like inks with a pen in combination ink-drawing-and-wash. Mixed or used in conjunction with the opaque colors and white, the effects of gouache may be accomplished. Underdrawings of charcoal or water-soluble inks may be incorpo-

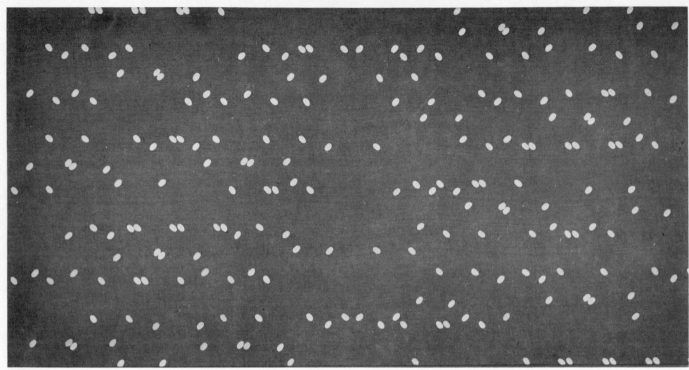

Above is *Han-San Cadence* by Larry Poons, done with acrylics and fabric dye on canvas. Below, *Saraband*, an acrylic on canvas by Morris Louis. Each of these paintings (which measure 12 feet in width) in its own way suggests visual music.

Contemporary artists frequently combine painting and sculpture in a single art form. Illustrated is Richard Smith's *Envelopes,* done in acrylics on shaped canvas.

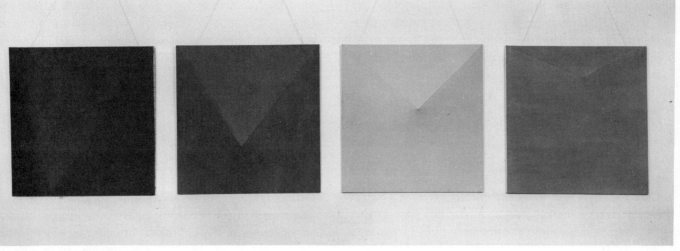

RICHARD FEIGEN GALLERY, NEW YORK

rated into the painting. If these are sprayed with matte medium (which, thinned, may be used with an atomizer as described in the section on fixative for pastels (page 139), they will not bleed or smear when paint is applied over them.

The synthetic paints may be used like tempera, and a number of the major artists who have long worked in tempera have now taken up the synthetics, which produce similar results without the laborious and difficult traditional tempera procedure. The characteristic opalescence and luminosity of tempera can be achieved with the synthetics; transparent layers of color can be built up to a final effect of great depth of tone. Areas of opacity and translucence can be systematically developed, shadows and depth worked in with increasingly dark, transparent washes, light areas, and highlights being brought forward with opaque light colors. The effect of tempera may be arrived at by using polymer paints alone on a wood or Masonite panel prepared with a synthetic gesso ground. In addition, synthetic paints may be used with traditional egg-emulsion tempera. The egg yolk is prepared as for tempera (page 103), and the polymer colors are then mixed on the palette with the egg. The mixture should be about one-third egg to two-thirds pigment, and it is diluted to the desired transparency with a water-filled brush.

To achieve the heavy-bodied quality of casein, the polymer tube paints may be mixed with polymer matte medium and additives such as whiting or Celite. The proportions should be about one part additive to three parts paint-plus-medium.

The synthetics can act and look like oil paint too. The tube colors have about the same consistency and working qualities as tube oil paints; the synthetics that come in jars have a more liquid consistency, but adding gel (one part gel to no more than two parts paint) will give them the body of oils. If you want to use the synthetics exclusively in this way, you should choose the New Masters line, which was developed expressly for the purpose and handles — or "feels" — most like the traditional medium although, of course, it is used with water, like all the synthetic paints. The advantage it offers, as all the synthetics do, is that drying time is accelerated and work can proceed rapidly; a finished painting will dry completely in a few hours. The richness and depth of oil colors, the marvelous textural surface effects, the characteristic "resistance" and workability of the pigments, and the final glowing semi-lustrous

151

gloss of the surface are within the reach of the synthetic paints. The gel dries to a glossy finish. If you want a matte finish, you can either mix matte medium with the gel or, better, varnish the finished painting with matte medium. For high impasto or textural effects, use modeling paste; although it can be mixed with the colors, it is better to apply it to the support first and then paint over it.

You can use synthetics with any of the traditional media, but take particular care when using them with oils. Oil paint cannot be actually mixed with polymer. You can paint opaque oils or oil glazes over polymer as soon as it is dry, or polymer over an oil underpainting, but only after it has dried completely. And if you attempt this, keep the oil content of the oil paint as low as possible by thinning it considerably with turpentine.

All sorts of aggregates may be added to polymer paints to achieve textural effects. Such additives — sand, sawdust, marble dust, and so on — actually become part of the paint film. The aggregates should be soaked in polymer medium before being mixed with the colors so that they do not use up medium that is needed to form the paint film. Aggregates may also be sprinkled on top of the paint while it is still wet. When the paint is dry and the aggregate particles have adhered, apply a coat of matte or glossy medium to lock the particles in a polymer film.

Paper and pieces of fabric can also be glued to the surface of a painting to make a collage. Apply a coat of polymer medium (either matte or gloss) to the collage piece and to the area on the support to receive it, and press the piece in place while the medium is still wet. Lightweight, pliable materials such as tissue or gauze can be soaked in the polymer medium and draped or bunched on the surface to produce a three-dimensional effect; to attach heavier materials, such as cardboard or wood, use the gel. When the medium is thoroughly dry (which may take several hours if the collage materials are very absorbent and have soaked up a great deal of medium), further overpainting may be done.

The synthetic paints are a remarkable product of our technological age. The advantages they offer are so many and their flexibility is so great that they could conceivably eventually replace the traditional media altogether. At present, however, they stand beside the traditional media, and the artist may choose them or not, as it pleases him, and according to his purpose and personal style. But the synthetics can and should be used for the qualities that are uniquely their own: among these are a remarkable brilliance of color and an unparalleled luminosity. The artists using synthetics at this moment are exploring their many expressive possibilities, and the exploration will continue as each new painter takes them up, until the full range of possibilities has been discovered. And then, as the traditional media of painting still do, the synthetic paints will continue to offer an avenue of adventure to the artist.

Opposite, Russell Woody's *Sixth to Ninth Hour*. Liquitex was employed both as paint and as sculptural medium.

153

	Water-color	Fresco	Tempera	Oils
Alizarin Crimson	x			x
Aureolin (Cobalt) Yellow	x			x
Barium Yellow	x			x
Bianco Sangiovanni		x		
Blanc Fixe	x	x		
Burnt Sienna	x	x	x	x
Burnt Umber	x		x	x
Cadmium Orange	x		x	x
Cadmium Yellows	x		x	x
Cadmium Reds	x		x	x
Carbon Black			x	x
Cerulean Blue	x	x	x	x
Chinese White (Zinc White)	x			
Chromium-Oxide Green	x	x	x	x
Cobalt Blue	x	x	x	x
Cobalt Green	x	x		x
Cobalt (Arsenate) Violet Ⓣ	x	x		x
Cremnitz White Ⓣ				x
Flake White Ⓣ				x
Green Earth (*Terre Verte*)	x	x	x	x
Indian Red	x	x	x	x
Ivory Black	x		x	x
Lampblack	x	x	x	x
Manganese Blue	x	x		x
Mars Black	x	x	x	x
Mars Red	x	x	x	x
Mars Violet	x	x	x	x
Mars Yellow	x	x	x	x
Naples Yellow Ⓣ				x
Neutral *Blanc Fixe*		x		
Ocher	x	x	x	x
Phthalocyanine Blue	x		x	x
Phthalocyanine Green	x		x	x
Raw Sienna	x	x	x	x
Raw Umber	x	x	x	x
Red Oxides	x	x	x	x
Strontium Yellow	x			x
Titanium White	x	x	x	x
Transparent Yellow Ocher	x	x		x
Ultramarine Blue	x			x
Ultramarine Green	x			x
Vermilion				x
Viridian	x	x		x
Zinc White			x	x

Ⓣ — Toxic Pigment

Casein Palette   as listed for watercolor.

Encaustic Palette as listed for watercolor and oils.

Pastel Palette   as listed for watercolor, tempera, and oils,
excluding toxic pigments.

Permanent Pigments (Traditional Media)

Glossary

Aggregate. Inert particles such as sand or marble dust added to lime in making plaster. Aggregates may also be added to paint for textural effects.

Alla prima. The application of paint in a direct fashion, the brush-strokes final as made and not modified by glazes or scumbling.

Aquarelle. A name sometimes used to refer to watercolor used in its transparent form.

Arenato. The third of four layers of plaster applied to a wall that is to be frescoed.

Arriciato. The second of the four layers of plaster, sometimes called the equalizing layer, applied to a wall that is to be frescoed.

Bas-relief. A kind of sculpture in which the forms are attached to and project slightly from the background.

Binder. The substance in paint that holds the particles of pigment together and adheres them to the support when the paint is dry.

Bole. A red clay thinned with water. In tempera work, bole is applied on the gessoed panel in areas that are to receive gold leaf.

Bright. The type of paint brush in which short hairs or bristles are set in a flat ferrule.

Buon fresco. The form of fresco painting in which pigments in a water vehicle are applied to a freshly plastered section of wall while the plaster is still wet.

Canvas. A heavy textile of closely woven, relatively coarse fibers. The fibers may be jute, hemp, cotton, or flax (linen). The term is also used to refer to the support for a painting made of such a textile.

Cartoon. Generally, a full-size preliminary outline drawing or design for a composition.

Casein. A granular powder made from curd. Casein paint is made by mixing pigments with the casein powder and water.

Dammar varnish. A pale, lustrous varnish made from the resin of certain trees.

Diluent. The fluid added to paint to dilute it, as turpentine may be added to oils or water added to the egg-tempera emulsion.

Distemper. A water-base painting medium in which the binder is size (glue) rather than gum, as in watercolor.

Dowicide A. Trade name of a preservative (sodium orthophenyl phenate) added in small amounts to casein and gum solutions to retard spoilage.

Easel. A stand to hold a canvas, panel, drawing board, or other support in a convenient working position (generally vertical or nearly so).

Emulsion. A mixture of two liquids in which fine particles or globules of one are evenly dispersed in the other. An egg-and-water emulsion is used as the binder in traditional egg-tempera painting.

Encaustic. The painting medium in which pigments are mixed in a vehicle of dissolved or liquefied wax and fixed on the working surface by the application of heat.

Ferrule. The metal band that serves as a mount for the hairs or bristles of a paint brush and fastens them to the handle.

Filler. A fine, powdery inert substance such as marble dust, chalk, or talc added to paint to thicken or extend it. The filler is neutral and does not appreciably alter the color of the paint.

Fixative. A thin solution of varnish or shellac and a solvent used to fix or hold pigment particles (for instance, pastels) together and to the support.

Flat. The type of paint brush in which bristles or sable hairs of equal length are set in a ferrule that is flattened at the brush end. Bristle flats are used primarly in oil painting; sable flats are made for use with watercolor as well as oils.

Fresco. The painting medium in which pigments in a water vehicle are applied to a damp plastered wall. (See *buon fresco* and *fresco secco*.)

Fresco secco. The form of fresco painting in which pigments, in a vehicle of limewater or casein solution, are applied to a plastered wall that has been dampened just prior to painting.

Gesso. A ground made from an inert white substance such as gypsum or whiting and a glue solution.

Glaze. In painting, a layer of transparent paint that modifies the layer or layers of colors underneath.

Gouache. Watercolor that has been rendered opaque by the addition of a white pigment.

Ground. A base coat or coats of a substance such as gesso applied to a support to prepare it for the paint layer.

Impasto. The technique of applying a paint thickly so as to create a textured surface.

Intonaco. The last of the four layers of plaster applied to a wall that is to be frescoed. The painting is done on the *intonaco.*

Masonite. Trade name of a wallboard manufactured from wood that has been reduced to pulp under steam pressure and then pressed into sheets with heat. Masonite may be used whenever a panel support is desired.

Mastic varnish. A light-colored, glossy varnish for pictures made from mastic (a resin) and turpentine.

Matte. A surface texture that is uniformly dull as opposed to glossy.

Medium. The substance used by the artist to execute his painting (e.g., fresco and tempera are two traditional media). Medium is often used also to refer to the vehicle or liquid in which pigments are mixed.

Monochrome. Painting or drawing done in various values and intensities of a single color.

Oil paint. The painting medium in which pigments are mixed in an oil vehicle. Linseed oil is most commonly used.

Painting knife. A spatula with a flexible, triangular-shaped blade offset on a long shank. The painting knife is used, like the brush, to apply paint to a support.

Palette. In one meaning, the surface on which an artist lays out and mixes colors before applying them to a painting. In another meaning, the palette is the assortment of pigments that may be used with a particular medium. The term may also be used to refer to the specific colors used in a particular painting or preferred by a given artist or school of artists.

Palette knife. A spatula with a flexible, nearly straight blade. The blade generally is slightly wider than the handle and tapers slightly to a rounded tip. It is used primarily for mixing pigments and scraping paint off the palette.

Panel. A rigid support, traditionally of wood, on which a painting is executed.

Pastels. The painting medium in which dry pigments are pressed into sticks, usually with a small amount of a substance such as gum tragacanth as binder.

Pouncing. A method for transferring a full-scale design (cartoon) for a painting to the final working surface. The lines of the design, which is usually drawn on paper, are perforated with a tracing wheel. The drawing is then placed against the working surface, and a bag filled with a substance such as fine charcoal dust (called a pounce bag) is tapped along the lines. The dust filters through the perforations and, when the cartoon is removed, leaves a dotted line version of the original design.

Priming. The coat or coats of some substance, such as gesso or paint, applied to a support to prepare it for the paint layer.

Round. The type of paint brush in which the hairs or bristles are set in a round ferrule and gathered so that they taper toward the tip.

Scumbling. The process of scrubbing an opaque color over another, usually darker, color to modify it.

Sinopia. In Renaissance *buon fresco,* the full-scale sketch of the composition painted in a reddish brown pigment on the next-to-last (*arenato*) layer of plaster. As each portion of the final coat of plaster was applied, the part of the sinopia that was covered was redrawn from memory and frescoed.

Size. Broadly used, a glue, starch, gum, or other substance used to fill a porous surface. Size made of animal glue is applied to raw canvas to protect it from the harmful effects of oil paint.

Slaked lime (calcium hydrate). The product formed by adding water to quicklime. This hydrated lime is used in the preparation of fine plaster.

Solvent. The fluid, generally a volatile organic compound, used to thin paints to the desired working consistency and to clean brushes and equipment.

Stand oil. Polymerized linseed oil particularly useful in oil paints and glazes and in varnishes.

Support. The physical structure (paper, canvas, panel, etc.) that holds the ground (if any) and paint film of a painting.

Synthetics. Paints made from acrylic and vinyl resins that have been polymerized.

Tempera. The painting medium in which the pigments are mixed with an emulsion.

Trompe l'oeil. A manner of painting in which the two-dimensional surface is designed (by means of perspective, color, and modeling) to appear three-dimensional.

Trullisatio. The first of the four layers of plaster applied to a wall that is to be frescoed.

Turpentine. A solvent used by painters to thin oil paint and in making varnishes. Grades suitable for the artist's use are labeled either "rectified" or "pure gum spirits of turpentine."

Varnish. A substance made from resin and used in painting as a protective coating over the paint layers (and occasionally between the layers).

Vehicle. The liquid in which pigments are mixed for application to the painting surface.

Wash. Paint generously diluted and applied smoothly over a broad area.

Watercolor. Broadly, painting media in which pigments are mixed in a water vehicle. The term may also be used specifically to refer to transparent watercolor as opposed to gouache and distemper.

Bibliography

Chaet, Bernard. *Artists at Work.* Cambridge, Mass.: Webb Books 1960.

Csoka, Stephen. *Pastel Painting: Modern Techniques.* New York: Reinhold, 1962.

Eastlake, Sir Charles Lock. *Materials for a History of Oil Painting* London: Vol. I, 1847, Vol. II, 1869. New York: Dover, 1960.

Fiene, Ernest. *Complete Guide to Oil Painting.* New York: Watson-Guptill, 1964.

Gettens, Rutherford J., and Stout, George L. *Painting Materials. A Short Encyclopedia.* New York: Van Nostrand, 1942. Dover, 1966.

Holt, Elizabeth Gilmore. *The Literary Sources of Art History.* Princeton: Princeton University Press, 1947. Paperback edition: *A Documentary History of Art,* Vols. I and II. New York: Doubleday, 1958.

Kautzky, Ted. *Ways with Watercolor,* 2nd ed. New York: Reinhold, 1963.

Kay, Reed. *The Painter's Companion.* Cambridge, Mass.: Webb Books, 1961.

Mayer, Ralph. *The Artist's Handbook of Materials and Techniques.* New York: Viking Press, 1940.

Nicolaides, Kimon. *The Natural Way to Draw.* Boston: Houghton Mifflin, 1941.

Potter, Eric. *Painters on Painting.* New York: Grosset and Dunlap, 1963.

Pratt, Francis, and Fizell, Becca. *Encaustic: Materials and Methods.* New York: Lear, 1949.

Taubes, Frederic. *Painting Materials and Techniques.* New York: Watson-Guptill, 1964.

Thompson, Daniel V. *The Materials and Techniques of Medieval Painting.* London: 1936. New York: Dover, 1956.

————. *The Practice of Tempera Painting.* New Haven: Yale University Press, 1936. New York: Dover, 1962.

Woody, Russell O. *Painting with Synthetic Media.* New York: Reinhold, 1965.